LOVING

AD♡PTED

CHILDREN

WELL

LOVING

AD♡PTED

CHILDREN

WELL

A 5 Love Languages® Approach

GARY CHAPMAN, PhD
and LAUREL SHALER, PhD

NORTHFIELD PUBLISHING

CHICAGO

Published in association with the Hartline Literary Agency, Pittsburgh, PA.

Names and details of some stories have been changed to protect the privacy of individuals.

Edited by Amanda Cleary Eastep
Interior design: Erik M. Peterson
Cover design: Kaylee Dunn

Library of Congress Cataloging-in-Publication Data

Names: Chapman, Gary D., 1938- author. | Shaler, Laurel, author.
Title: Loving adopted children well : a 5 love languages approach / Gary Chapman and Laurel Shaler.
Description: Chicago : Moody Publishers, 2024. | Includes bibliographical references. | Summary: "Adoption brings unique challenges. Love and bonding don't always come naturally. There can be emotional distress, frustration, and disappointment. With empathy for adoptive parents, Chapman and Shaler provide an honest and invaluable resource of wisdom, joy, and healing. Apply these lessons and watch love grow and flourish in your home"-- Provided by publisher.
Identifiers: LCCN 2023030473 (print) | LCCN 2023030474 (ebook) | ISBN 9780802431875 (paperback) | ISBN 9780802472861 (ebook)
Subjects: LCSH: Adoption. | Adoptees. | Adoptive parents.
Classification: LCC HV874.8 .C435 2024 (print) | LCC HV874.8 (ebook) | DDC 362.734--dc23/eng/20230926
LC record available at https://lccn.loc.gov/2023030473
LC ebook record available at https://lccn.loc.gov/2023030474

We hope you enjoy this book from Northfield Publishing. Our goal is to provide high-quality, thought-provoking books and products that connect truth to your real needs and challenges. For more information on other books and products that will help you with all your important relationships, go to northfieldpublishing.com or write to:

Northfield Publishing
820 N. LaSalle Boulevard
Chicago, IL 60610

1 3 5 7 9 10 8 6 4 2

Printed in the United States of America

From Dr. Laurel Shaler:
In honor of my precious children, my "why" for this book.
I pray I show you all the love you deserve, that you forgive me
when I fail, and that you know that as much as I love you,
Jesus loves you even more.

In memory of my beloved daddy, whose unconditional love
I will carry with me all the days of my life until we meet again.
And in loving memory of my brother, Jake.
Pals forever.

And in memory of H.W. for her selfless love.

From Dr. Gary Chapman:
Dedicated to the many parents who have chosen to adopt
children who needed a loving family. Few decisions are more
rewarding and challenging. May you find this book
a welcome companion on the journey.

Contents

Introduction:
A Word from Gary

A NUMBER OF YEARS AGO, I coauthored a book with Dr. Ross Campbell titled *The 5 Love Languages of Children: The Secret to Loving Children Effectively*. The book has sold over two million copies and has helped many parents learn how to effectively meet a child's need for emotional love. The question for parents is not: Do you love your child? The question is: Does your child feel loved? Discovering a child's "primary" love language and speaking it regularly connects deeply with the child's need for love.

I am not suggesting that you speak only the child's "primary" love language. We want to speak all five love languages, so the child learns how to receive and give love in all five languages. However, if we do not give heavy doses of the child's primary love language, the child will not feel loved even though we express love in the other languages.

Through the years, adoptive parents have often asked, "Does this work with adopted children? After all, we don't have the biological bonding with our adopted child. Are there insights that will help us effectively love our adopted children?"

When Dr. Laurel Shaler contacted me about writing a book on how the five love languages can help adoptive parents, I was immediately interested. When I found out that she and her husband have two adopted children and that she is a university professor in the field of counselor education, I was convinced that she was the one I should partner with in writing the book you hold in your hands.

I have always written out of my own experience and what I have learned in counseling couples and families for over forty years. However, I have had no experience in raising adopted children and limited experience in counseling adoptive parents. Therefore, this book is largely written by Dr. Shaler. I have critiqued and made suggestions along the journey, but I am deeply excited for you to hear her voice of real-life experience.

Loving Adopted Children Well will answer the question: How do the five love languages work when rearing adopted children? For those who are adoptive parents, or considering adopting a child, as well as counselors or pastors who seek to help adoptive parents, I think you will find this book a welcome companion.

— GARY CHAPMAN, PhD, coauthor of *The 5 Love Languages of Children: The Secret to Loving Children Effectively*

1

Loving Intentionally

I (LAUREL) PULLED UP to a house with the longest driveway I'd had ever seen. Noticing a pony meandering through the large front field, my husband, Nick, and I double-checked the address. We were surprised to learn we were, in fact, at the correct home. Feeling simultaneously excited and nervous, we slowly made our way down that seemingly never-ending stretch of pavement with great anticipation. We parked the car and walked up to the front door, knots in our stomachs and our hearts pounding.

Before we had even knocked, the big brown door opened. On the other side stood a lovely older woman (she'd hate me for calling her older), holding a baby. As I stepped over the threshold, she placed that little girl in my arms. In that moment, I knew—*I knew*—we were meant for each other. The rest, as they say, is history. And it is history in the making. Our adoption story is nothing short of amazing, and I'll share more of that story (and the second one!) in a bit.

ADOPTION BASICS

The two children we adopted—forevermore *our* children—are two of the approximately 120,000 children adopted annually in the United States.[1] The majority of these children are five years or younger at the time of their adoption. Our daughter was two months and five days old on the mild February day we met her. The baby boy who followed a few years later was a mere three days old. Perhaps you can relate to adopting a young child. Or maybe you are still in the considering and praying phase. It could be that you counsel, pastor, or simply want to support adoptive families. Adoptive families are more common than some believe, with one in twenty-five families having at least one adopted child and one in fifty children having been adopted.[2] This equates to about 1.5 million children living in the United States right now who have been adopted, or about 2 percent of the population. In whatever way you have been or will be impacted by adoption, this book is for you.

Adoption is no longer the secret act it once was. Not only are there more open adoptions between birth families and adoptive families than in the past, but adoptive children are now more likely to know about their start in life. As you may know, an open adoption is one in which the birth or biological family (these terms are often used interchangeably), or at a minimum the birth mother and the adoptive parent(s), have some degree of knowledge about one another. This might even include meeting in person. In fact, some adoptive parents are in the delivery room as the child who is being placed with them is born. Sometimes, an open adoption only includes using first names; while other times, more information, such as last names and contact information, is shared. While the degree of openness varies, the birth family and adoptive family often keep in touch with each other as the child grows up. That could be through pictures and letters, or it might involve occasional visits. An open adoption typically involves the biological family and the adoptive family communicating without an intermediary, whereas a semi-open adoption often involves the use of the adoption agency or attorney to communicate between the two parties and does not always include the sharing of identifying information.

A closed adoption means there is no known identifying information shared between the two parties, the placing parent(s) and the receiving parent(s), and there is no contact between the families. In our family's case, we do not have any kind of relationship or communication with the birth family of one of our children (I met the birth mother only one time). With the other child, we keep in close contact with a couple of biological relatives, but not the birth parents. Sometimes, the level of openness changes and evolves as time passes. I have even heard one birth mother who speaks frequently about her story share that her teenage biological child regularly spends the night in her home. The primary focus must always be on the child or children and for their benefit. They need to be safe and secure, emotionally and physically. As a family, we are attempting to weave our children's adoption stories into their lives in an age-appropriate and sensitive way so as to be honest, but not overwhelm them. On one occasion, after sharing some new information about her adoption with my daughter, she wisely said (at the ripe old age of five years old), "That is a little difficult to understand, but also educational." We'll keep sharing as she matures and is ready to learn more. Most importantly, we want our children to know that they are deeply loved by many people, regardless of how their adoptions came to be.

WHY ADOPT?

People come to adoption for many different reasons. While we have experienced infertility, we actually felt called by God to adopt *prior* to knowing that—barring any medical intervention—we could not conceive naturally. My desire was to become a mother, to parent a child or children, not necessarily to be pregnant, give birth, or have biological/birth children (though I was always open to that if the Lord willed). We didn't know what the Lord had in store for us, but we were not in any hurry. After nine years of marriage, we answered the call to pursue adoption, though we would surpass our fourteenth wedding anniversary before our first adoption was finalized.

Other couples decide on adoption specifically after experiencing infertility. Many couples suffer tremendous pain due to the inability to conceive. I have known women who cried each month when they discovered once again that they were not pregnant. Sometimes, a pregnancy takes place but does not result in the live birth of a child. It is a well-known statistic that, sadly, almost one in three pregnancies ends in miscarriage. This heartache can complicate the adoption process. As authors Graham and Dormon note, it is important to emotionally deal with the infertility prior to starting the adoption journey.[3] That does not mean the disappointment will ever completely go away, but working on accepting what you have not been able to change is important. Even if you have already adopted but are still dealing with the searing loss of infertility or miscarriage, please consider counseling. This might need to include couples counseling, as such a loss can take a tremendous toll on a marriage as well. A troubled marriage is not healthy ground to build a family on, so please do seek marriage counseling as soon as possible.

For others, adoption is part of the building of their family, but not the entire picture. In these cases, the adopted child or children join a couple's own biological children. I know people who specifically pursued adoption without ever attempting to have their own biological children; some of these are single individuals.

No matter why you, or someone you love, have arrived at the choice to adopt, "adoption is the heart of God."[4] This is revealed in at least two ways. The first is that God deeply cares about orphans, often described as the fatherless in the Bible. The second—and more important—way is that God adopts us as His children when we accept the free gift of salvation provided through His Son, Jesus Christ. Below are a few verses that speak to this:

> "He executes justice for the fatherless." (Deuteronomy 10:18 ESV)

> "A father to the fatherless . . . is God." (Psalm 68:5)

> "But when the set time had fully come, God sent his Son, born of a woman, born under the law, to redeem those under the law, so that we might receive adoption to sonship." (Galatians 4:4–5)

> "Religion that is pure and undefiled before God the Father is this: to visit orphans and widows in their affliction, and to keep oneself unstained from the world." (James 1:27 ESV)

Adoption should never be looked at as a backup plan to having biological children. Yes, the Lord sometimes uses infertility to bring couples to the point of adopting, but in His sovereignty, adoption was His plan all along. It can be hard to wrap our heads and hearts around this. We know that God created Adam and Eve and, blessing them, told them to "be fruitful and increase in number."[5] We know that God's heart is for nuclear families to stay together and for children to stay with their biological parents whenever possible.

Yet, for a myriad of reasons, it's not always possible. Sometimes parents decide to place a child for adoption for reasons such as the parent's age, financial difficulties, or circumstances surrounding conception. Sometimes parents die or are harmful, resulting in the child or children being placed for adoption. And sometimes biological parents, as a result of in vitro fertilization (IVF) producing a significant number of embryos, cannot carry or raise all of these children. Thank God that in those instances there are families able and willing to care for these children through embryo adoption. In this situation, an adoptive mother will have an embryo transferred into her own uterus, thereby carrying and giving birth to her adopted child—becoming both the birth mother and the adoptive mother. At the time of this writing, my husband and I have gone through an embryo adoption ourselves and are awaiting the arrival of our third baby, due very soon!

Adoption may not be Plan A in our minds, but it is never Plan B in God's mind. We can't always understand His ways, but as my pastor Barry Jimmerson says, "God can hit straight with a crooked stick!"

THE IMPACT OF ADOPTION

I mentioned that our adoption history is in the making. The adoptions are completed, over and done with as soon as the judge's gavel hit the desk with a resounding thud. The words "It is so ordered" remain some of the most exciting words that have ever been spoken to me in my entire life. Yet, the impact of adoption—the good and the bad, the pros and the cons, the love and the loss—is never-ending. Nancy Newton Verrier, author of *The Primal Wound: Understanding the Adopted Child*, wrote that adoptive parents "who have been waiting for a baby and who feel ready to love and nurture" come into the adoption "picture at a disadvantage."[6]

To begin with, my children were conceived by couples who do not share my husband's DNA or mine. I didn't even meet one birth mom, and the other was only a few weeks shy of delivery when we first met. The decisions they made resulted in our children having a challenging start to life. It would be easy to say—and easier to live—but is simply untrue that solely because we met our children when they were itty-bitty and have devotedly cared for them, their adoption status is water under the bridge. No, the story continues. While it doesn't have to always be at the forefront, it also can never be forgotten or ignored. Even children adopted as infants (when the baby is taken home from the hospital by their new parents) have experienced trauma. Being removed from biological parents, regardless of the child's age, is the primary wound Verrier is referring to. Yes, children can be resilient and overcome many challenges, but nothing changes the fact that the trauma happened.

I recall a time when one of my children was struggling with managing emotions and behavior. As I started to chat with a trusted friend and pondered whether this could potentially be related to the adoption status, my friend blew off my notion with a wave of her hand. "Nah . . . all children act like this." Sometimes this is true, but sometimes it's not. Sorting through what is and what isn't adoption related can be complex, but it always needs to be considered. Additionally, it's crucial to connect with other adoptive parents. In the story I just shared, I neglected to do that.

Thankfully, we have been able to connect with other families similar to ours. In fact, our daughter attended preschool and kindergarten at a school that happened to have several adopted children in her age group. We didn't know that when we selected the school, but the Lord did. Another friend who adopted several children is farther along in her journey than our family, and I have relied heavily on her at times as I've sorted through how best to approach adoption-related topics with my children. We need the support of other adoptive families, and adoptive families need the support of the community at large. There are many who are adoptive- and trauma-informed who have not personally adopted. The bottom line is how crucial support is for adoptive families. We'll talk more about that later in the book.

MORE OF OUR STORY

I promised more of our journey to adoption, so here it is: The woman holding the baby girl in the opening paragraph of this chapter was her biological relative who had sacrificially agreed to take her home from the hospital and care for her, and who also sought out a loving adoptive family. She knew that she and her husband were too advanced in age to provide the kind of family she wanted that little one to have, and she was also bound and determined to fiercely protect that child. In a series of events that could only have been orchestrated by God (because our efforts over several years and just as many adoption agencies produced nothing but heartache), we wound up at her doorstep.

I still find it hard to believe, but I lived it, so I know it's true! One Wednesday night at church, the same church I had attended since I was four years old, one of my childhood Sunday school teachers came up to me and said, "I know a lady who is looking for an adoptive family for her relative. Can I give her your phone number?" Not giving it much thought (because we had been down that road with others before), I assured her that was fine, while doubting anything would come of it. Two days later, as I was pulling into the gym parking lot, my phone rang. I didn't recognize the number but answered anyway. It was her! The baby's relative had called after all. Another two days passed, and there we were, holding the baby girl who would legally become ours later that year.

A lot happened between that February and November when the adoption was finalized (fittingly, in National Adoption Month), but we got there. We tried to enjoy the time we had with that little girl, never knowing during those months whether the adoption would go through. Regardless, we made her a part of every aspect of our life. We introduced her to our families, and she was with us on holidays, birthday celebrations, and vacations. Yet, she was not with us full-time until we were given custody. Once we were granted custody and finalized the adoption a few months later, the hard work of parenting really began. It brings to mind what my beloved daddy told me when we shared our initial plans to adopt. He said, "Parenting is the hard part, and I know you'll do it well." His faith in me and his utter devotion to my children until the day he died carried me far in this adoption journey.

TESTIMONIAL TIME

It's so important to have people who believe in you, in *this*. People who can talk openly with you; people you can cry with. I shed many tears during the wait to adopt, begging God to fulfill my longing and also wrestling with God over why children were being abused and neglected when I could give a child a loving and safe life. As the months passed without us knowing if the little girl we were helping care for would become our daughter, I would rock her and sing "You Are My Sunshine." Every time I got to the last line—you know the one, "Please don't take my sunshine away"—I would choke back tears. But the tears didn't stop after the adoptions were finalized. More were shed as I have struggled to best help my children and lamented over parenting decisions I have made.

Adoptive families need others to come alongside us, and it's awfully helpful when they have been there themselves. That is a major reason for writing this book and offering it as a resource to you. We'll touch more on the nature of this book in chapter 2. First, we'd like to share a few encouraging words from adult adoptees. Whether you are just starting the adoption process or are in the thick of parenting, we hope hearing from adult adoptees who have had positive adoption experiences gives you some hope that even though parenting children who have been adopted has its challenges—and the adoptees certainly have a mixed bag of emotions—it is worth it for all involved. While not every adoptee has a positive story, many do, and they are worth sharing.

These stories are being retold with permission from those who openly shared about their experiences.

Amanda

Now an adult, Amanda, at the age of seventeen, shared about her childhood experience of being adopted. She said that when she was first adopted, she did "not know that a mother and father were people who loved you and helped you."[7] She went on to write that she did not even know what the word *love* meant! Of course, this was no fault of her own, as she hadn't ever really been shown love. Yet, in time, she came to understand love as demonstrated by the mom and dad who adopted her. She wisely wrote these profound words:

> To parents who may adopt or have adopted, I think the most important thing is not to give up on the child, and no matter what, don't stop loving them. What they need most, whether they realize it or not, is love. That is the best thing you can do for that child. If they push you away, show them more love.[8]

Drew

Drew was adopted in the early 1980s, the only child of the husband and wife who became his parents. He grew up in an area without many other children who had the same experience of being adopted. In fact, when he was young, he was frequently identified by his status as an adopted child. Although "othered"— or treated as different—at times by members of his community, he states, "My parents provided a great life." He also had a close relationship with his grandparents, who were an integral part of his childhood.

When Drew was sharing his story, there was one line that brought me to tears. When asked how he knew he was loved, he replied, "That could take a million pages to answer, I suppose." He knew he was loved because his parents and grandparents made time for him, they took him fishing and to football games, they taught him kindness, they sang to him, they told him stories, and they took him to church. Drew also expressed appreciation for his biological mother, who he said loved him and chose to place him for adoption to "have a better life." He said that if he could say one thing to her, it would be "Thank you." What a powerful story.

Patricia

Patricia was born in Germany at the end of World War II and was adopted at six months old from an orphanage by an American couple. Like many other orphans, Patricia was not cared for as she should have been prior to being adopted and has always been grateful for the life she was given by her parents. Patricia "always wanted to help other orphaned little girls because of what her adopted parents had done for her." She and her husband, Ernie, took in three foster daughters, one of whom they adopted. They have also been very involved in foster care advocacy (since the mid-1980s!) and training others in the Trust-Based Relational Intervention (TBRI) approach. (More to come on that in a later chapter.) Like Drew, Patricia expresses gratitude for the parents who adopted her.

Sophie

Sophie was born in Russia and adopted at the age of one. Sophie shared this: "My mom says my birth mom is her hero. My mom is *my* hero because she loved me enough to come get me. She has shown a lot of love in her support. She has taken time for me and my sister. She prays with us. She thanks God every day for us. Having a parent who thanks God for us is so nice!"

Sophie also related that her parents are supportive in both big and small ways. One small example is when she receives a text from one of them that says something as simple as "Have a great day. I love you."

Sophie, age eighteen at the time of this writing, has never doubted her parents' love.

MY PRAYER

Not long ago, as I was telling my daughter good night, we embraced for one final hug before lights out. With her little arms clinging to my neck and her head on my shoulder, she said sweetly, "You're the best mother in the whole world, and I promise to love you forever." Now, I know the first part isn't true. I'm not a perfect parent and would say that if anyone promises you perfection if you just say or do *x*, *y*, or *z*—run! So, I'm not the best mother in the whole world.

The fact that she thinks that is true is precious to me, and it motivates me to continue striving to be the best mother I can be for *her*. I don't know what things will look like when my children grow up and become "adult adoptees," but I sincerely hope we have a success story like the others that have been shared in this chapter. One day my daughter will realize I am not the best mother in the world, but I do pray she and her siblings will always love me—and I most assuredly will love them with every breath I breathe for as long as I live.

WRAPPING UP CHAPTER ONE

As my daughter started to take a bite of a fruit I'm allergic to, I started to tell her not to eat it, fearing she would have a negative reaction. Then, I remembered that since we are not biologically related, I had no reason to believe she would be allergic to the same fruit. Although we might briefly forget, we can never completely forget that our children are adopted, nor should we want to. We have chosen to adopt children, and this part of their story—of our story—will remain with us throughout our lives. This is a love we can intentionally grow bit by bit and develop into a love that will last forever.

Regardless of the lack of biological connection, and the fact that I am her mother and not her sister, my little girl thinks we're pretty much twins. I recall a time we went on a mother-daughter camping trip. By "camping," I mean we stayed in a lodge that had a private bathroom. So, closer to "glamping." The room we were staying in was designed for a family and contained a queen-size bed and two sets of bunk beds. Despite all the bed options, my daughter told me we needed to sleep together in one of the twin beds "because we're twins, and that's why they make twin beds." She knows she is adopted, but that doesn't stop her from viewing us as being "two peas in a pod" due to the attachment we have developed. Fortunately, I was able to convince her that since we are both queens, the queen bed would work out better for us than the little twin bed.

Adoption is not easy, but it can have a lifelong, positive impact for both the child and the parents. In the next chapter, we'll explore how this book can help you along this parenting journey.

2

Why *This* Book?

AS A LICENSED mental health professional, as well as a professor, I've been through many education and continuing education programs. When I became a mama myself, my desire to grow my knowledge and become excellent in parenting grew voraciously. Probably unreasonably so. Nevertheless, I read all the books and raced through many training programs. One of my favorite resources was based on the wildly successful book *The 5 Love Languages: The Secret to Love That Lasts*, by Dr. Gary Chapman.[1] Dr. Chapman took those concepts and applied them to parenting, resulting in another best-selling book, *The 5 Love Languages of Children: The Secret to Loving Children Effectively* (coauthored with Dr. Ross Campbell).[2]

One of the most impactful points to me was discovering that young children need lots of love born out of each of the five love languages, which are:

Acts of Service—doing things for our children
Gifts—gifts that are appropriate to the child's age
Physical Touch—affirming touches
Quality Time—giving the child our undivided attention
Words of Affirmation—verbalizing encouraging words

While I was already using each of these, there were important nuances I discovered. For example, all parents are well aware of the many acts of service we provide to our children. Oh, the endless acts of service! We bathe them, diaper them, dress them, feed them. And in order to do any of those things, we spend money on them to purchase necessities like food, diapers, clothes . . . and all those toys (how many stuffed animals does one child need?). As they grow and develop, we want them to become more independent. Of course, this is a necessary and important life skill, and I want this for my children as much as every other parent does. More than anything, I want my son to finish potty training! Yet, there are times when a parent can choose to provide an act of service to a child who is able do that thing for themselves. I recall several times when my daughter—who could certainly put on her shoes—asked for my help. With an open heart, I received the message that it meant something to her emotionally for me to assist her in this small way. So, I would have her sit on the loveseat and show her love through this seemingly insignificant act. The reality is that it was not insignificant to her.

In reading through Drs. Chapman and Campbell's helpful book on loving children well and applying the concepts in the parenting of my children, these questions occurred to me:

How could I apply the love languages to the children the Lord provided to our family through adoption?

Could the love languages look different when applied to other adoptive families as well? If so, how?

One example is the idea of the love language of Gifts. While many families (especially those grandmas and aunts) spoil new babies born into the family, how might a child who has been adopted perceive and receive gifts? Might they view the gift giving as an attempt to make up for what they've lost or an effort to buy their love? Could a child feel manipulated? While the toddler dragging around the toy puppy might not have these thoughts, is it possible he will later in life? Or perhaps the parent starts to question whether the child is being spoiled to the child's detriment, simply because the parent is using the power of the purchase to try to overcome guilt over something the child has been through or to help ease the child's sadness.

As I worked my way through the application of the five love languages to children, and through some of the other chapters (such as those on discipline and anger), I discovered more and more helpful content that I believed could be applied in adoptive families. And I believed that families like ours would benefit from some modifications and concrete examples.

In teaming up with Dr. Chapman to write this book, we seek to apply the five love languages in a way that helps adoptive families and those who support them. We'll share stories that provide clear and helpful illustrations and offer you hope and resources for your own adoption journey. More than anything, our desire is for children who have been adopted to really feel loved. By providing helpful tips and practical applications for those of you raising adopted children, we hope to enable you to powerfully demonstrate this love.

WHAT YOU CAN EXPECT

You likely picked up this book because you are in an adoptive family or know an adoptive family *and* because you are familiar with the five love languages. If you are not very familiar with them, don't worry, we'll cover them thoroughly as we go. As previously noted, the five love languages are Acts of Service, Gifts, Physical Touch, Quality Time, and Words of Affirmation. In this book, these will be tailored toward adoptive families. As we cover each, we'll also touch on adoption-related topics such as attachment, understanding adopted children, co-parenting, solo parenting, sibling rivalry, and more. All through the lens of adoptive families, not to make those of us who gratefully fall into this category feel different, but to be honest and helpful about both the challenges and possible solutions.

Addressing some presuppositions will help you as you read through this book: First, the terms *child* and *children* are both used knowing some readers will have one child by adoption and some will have more than one. Second, we believe in using people-first language. While it's preferable to avoid preceding *parent* or *child* with the word *adoptive*, those terms are used often in this book, simply for the sake of clarity. In the real world, these are just parents and children. It can actually be quite offensive to be referred to as an adoptive parent or an adopted child, except when it is necessary. In addition, this book primarily references couples rather than solo parents. We know and recognize that there are many single people parenting adopted children. Sometimes it is due to divorce, sometimes it is due to the death of one parent, and sometimes it is due to a single person adopting solo. We will look at single parenting more in-depth in a later chapter, as well as in a chapter on supporting adoptive families.

Finally, we want to note that there are seemingly countless books on parenting, yet the focus of this one is solely on loving children who have been adopted and supporting families touched by adoption. While parenting definitely involves discipline, this book does not cover that topic (or many other worthwhile topics). We want to keep our focus homed in on the topic of love because we know it will undoubtedly help relationships get better, deeper, and stronger. A close and healthy relationship between a parent and a child goes a long way in navigating the many challenging aspects of parenting.

During this process of exploring the five love languages and related topics, you'll read some more stories that help illustrate what is being discussed. These stories will include real-life examples, told with permission, as well as fictional scenarios and composite stories. We'll share a case study that will be woven throughout the chapters on the love languages to serve as a kind of thread throughout the book. That case study is described next.

JACK AND RUTHIE: A CASE STUDY

Jack and Ruthie married right after college graduation. When asked when they might have a baby, their standard answer was "in a few years." The years passed, but that remained their answer. Their secret was that they had never prevented pregnancy. They longed for children, but didn't want to share that with others. Several years into their marriage, Ruthie finally saw two pink lines on her pregnancy test. She kept the positive test result to herself, planning a special way to share the major news with Jack. Sadly, the excitement was short lived as Ruthie experienced the devastation of a miscarriage.

After some time for physical and emotional healing, the couple decided to try again. They were not opposed to simple fertility measures to increase their chances but had no desire to use in vitro fertilization. After another unsuccessful year, Jack approached

Ruthie about the possibility of adoption. Ruthie had been exploring this option herself, but feared Jack would not be on board. Ruthie was thankful he was, and they began their pursuit. After exploring numerous adoption agencies, they settled on one and were quickly matched. They knew this didn't happen to everyone and were thrilled, until they suddenly stopped hearing from the birth mother. The agency notified them that the birth mother had changed her mind. This brought on another round of loss and grief for Ruthie and Jack, who were now fully committed to the process, even if it would be a long one.

In time, they were successfully matched, and they brought home a baby girl straight from the hospital. They named her Marlene after her grandmother. The first several months were a mixture of exhaustion and bliss, though Ruthie in particular still struggled with feelings of insecurity and loss over their prior experiences. The initial high of finally having a child in their home started to wear off, and there were some difficulties with bonding; however, those appeared to be overcome by the time Marlene was about eighteen months old.

Now that their daughter is four years old, she is acting out in ways that Ruthie and Jack struggle with knowing how to manage. Marlene vacillates between wanting to be cuddled constantly and not wanting to be touched, between needing help with everything and not wanting help with anything. She used to get excited when her mom brought her a gift, but now those get tossed to the side. Ruthie and Jack are trying to sort through how to balance time with Marlene with their jobs and another adoption. They thought that Marlene knew she was loved—they've attempted to tell her and show her in lots of different ways, but nothing seems to stick. Now what? they wonder.

The first thing that needs to happen is for Ruthie and Jack to get on the same parenting page. We'll cover that a little later in the book, but before we do, we'll take a deeper dive into what adoptive families can do when they don't initially *feel* love for their children. We'll look into that topic in the next chapter, and we'll loop back around to Ruthie and Jack. From there, we'll explore the five love languages in the context of adoptive families. At the conclusion of each of those chapters, the case study of Ruthie, Jack, and Marlene will be used to further illustrate how the love language described in that chapter can be utilized with an adoptive family.

WHAT MAKES A PARENT A "REAL" PARENT

When my own daughter was four, I wanted to learn a little bit about what she was thinking related to adoption. So, I asked her this question: "What makes a mommy a real mommy?" Her simple and honest reply was this: "She is loving and kind." Adoptive parents might think they have to overcompensate for whatever their child has gone through. We might tend to spoil our children or feel an extra measure of guilt. (I can't speak for daddies, but mommy guilt is a real thing!) Nevertheless, I believe what our children want the most was best articulated by my sweet girl.

We should be loving and kind in the way we act toward and interact with our children. This can be shown through our acts of service, gifts, physical touch, quality time, and words of affirmation. Our prayer is that this book is an invaluable resource to adoptive families (and their loved ones) as it helps relieve the pressure and empowers you as you seek and strive to be the parent

God has called you to be—not perfect, but planned. As adult adoptee Brandy Leyva says of the parents who adopted her, "This is my mom. This is my dad. This is who they were created to be."[3]

3

When You Don't "Feel the Love"

MUCH LIKE THE CROSS of Jesus Christ, adoption is always a place where joy and sorrow meet. There is pain, loss, suffering; there is also tremendous blessing. My husband, Nick, and I experienced both deeply when it came time to meet and adopt our son.

JOY AND SORROW MEET

On a November day, as most of the world prepared for Thanksgiving while my father lay in a hospital bed after undergoing a stem cell transplant for leukemia, my husband and I told my parents the news. Our adoption attorney—the one who had helped us finalize our daughter's adoption—had recently called us. He related that he had been contacted by a young woman known to him who wished to place her child for adoption. Our attorney immediately thought of us, calling us to gauge our interest in meeting with the birth mom. (Because we know people have varying thoughts and opinions on how adoptive parents are selected, I'd like to clarify that our attorney did not have a list of waiting families at the time, and the young woman had asked him to choose—though I did meet with her before she made her final decision.) We were thrilled about the possibility of another adoption. Our family was not only deeply concerned about Daddy's health, but also experiencing inexpressible grief over the sudden loss of my older brother that previous July, only ten days after Daddy was diagnosed with cancer. I had never been in so much emotional pain in my life, and the thought of bringing a new life into our family gave us hope in the midst of tremendous sorrow.

The story, however, isn't wrapped up in a pretty blue bow. The time that elapsed between meeting a pregnant woman and meeting her birth son was a mere month. She delivered him early, and it was determined that he needed pediatric intensive care treatment due to prenatal exposure to some pretty toxic substances. All in the same day, as most people were preparing to celebrate New Year's Eve, we signed custody papers and met the baby boy who would become our son. It was no coincidence that I experienced one of the greatest joys of my life on the last night of the worst year of my life.

My husband and I took turns staying with our son in the pediatric intensive care unit while the other took care of our daughter. During my son's stay in the hospital, the little guy had some tough symptoms to contend with. Some, like sneezing, I would have never known to be associated with exposure to these substances. Other symptoms were more troublesome, like constant crying and needing a feeding tube. We quickly learned about neonatal abstinence syndrome (NAS), which happens when a baby exposed to drugs while in the womb is withdrawing from those substances. We also had to learn how to best help this baby boy. Certain aspects of caregiving, such as skin-to-skin contact, can help reduce hospital stays.[1] At the same time, some infants in this predicament are sensitive to touch.[2] Getting to know any newborn and learning their cues is challenging enough, but doing so when you are the adoptive mother and not the birth mother is even more complicated. Learning the most helpful ways to care for our son in this way was an unexpected challenge.

After a long and exhausting couple of weeks at the hospital, surrounded by amazing healthcare professionals, we were able to go home. We wore our favorite team's colors as they were playing in the college national championship that day. Before leaving the hospital, I cradled my baby while holding a photo of my beloved big brother and had my husband snap a photo. Then I cried tears of joy and sorrow on the way home. While the circumstances are all unique, many individuals and couples who are adopting experience their own joy and sorrow, and the children who are being adopted certainly endure this (even when they are too young to recognize or acknowledge it).

I believe we have to start with the presupposition that while most (I wish I could say all!) who adopt *desire* to love their children well, not all these parents *feel* the love. This can come as a surprise or a disappointment that needs to be addressed and worked through in order for a parent and child to bond. Even for those who do feel love from that first moment, as I experienced, not all are adequately prepared to demonstrate love in a manner that is the most helpful. Being prepared for what may come can help you adjust. If you are past that point but struggle with regrets, maybe understanding now what you were experiencing then will help alleviate some of your guilt. If you "felt more numb and scared than connected and competent,"[3] know that you are not alone—over half of parents in one survey reported these same feelings following the adoption of their children. By the way, many parents feel the same way after having biological children!

POST-ADOPTION DEPRESSION

Less than three months after our son was born, the COVID pandemic just about shut the world down. Like many other parents, we lost all childcare, so my husband and I took turns caring for the kids while the other worked. I worked from home and was there most of the time (except for my twice-daily walks to get out of the house). I was finding myself stressed out when it was my turn to watch both kiddos. Looking back, I realize I was struggling with anxiety at the time. Not only was I adjusting to life with both a daughter and a son, but we were in the midst of a pandemic. My husband had also received deployment orders, so we were preparing for that as well as experiencing the ongoing ups and downs of my father's cancer treatments. The worry that I dealt with is logical considering the challenging circumstances. Yet, even when adoptive parents are not facing all the "extra" stuff, they can experience mental health challenges following adoption, most often postpartum depression. One study comparing postpartum women to adoptive mothers found that the adoptive mothers had "comparable levels of depressive symptoms."[4] The women who had a history of infertility experienced "more depressive symptoms during the year following adoption."[5]

It's important for women who are planning to adopt or who have adopted recently to be aware of the potential for depressive symptoms and to seek professional help as soon as possible. Some symptoms to watch for include feeling down, thinking you should not have adopted, feeling guilty, or changes in appetite or sleep patterns (which may be hard to separate out from the lack of sleep most new parents experience). It's possible that these experiences might interfere with the bonding and attachment that takes place between parent and child, so getting help as soon as possible is good for not only the parent, but the child as well.

WHEN YOU LOVE YOUR CHILD
(BUT DON'T FEEL LOVING IN THE MOMENT)

John and Kristen have adopted two children. John shared that they loved both of their children from the start, but they didn't experience the emotional feeling of love in the beginning. John said it took him until his children were old enough to call him Daddy before he really started to accept himself as their father. John and Kristen learned to rely on each other, knowing that no one else in the world was going through their exact adoption process with their exact children. Part of how they coped with the occasional lack of *feeling* the love was to give the other partner permission to feel frustrated without judgment.

They also often prayed that the Lord would bind them together with their children and that God would increase their patience and love for each other and their children. John wants to remind other adoptive and would-be adoptive parents that even when love is not felt, parents must remind themselves what they already know about love. He said, "We know the journey that brought us to this point. We know we love our children. We know we love each other. We know the Lord orchestrated miracle after miracle to bring our family together. What we know must outweigh how we feel."

Another couple adopted three children from foster care, including two biological siblings. Jeanie says although a parent may not feel loving (which is normal), you make loving choices anyway. The more you do this, the more those loving feelings are cultivated. One of her primary ways of dealing with not feeling loving is through prayer—for the child, and also for God to give her love for her child that can only come through Him. Making time for herself also helps reduce exhaustion and discouragement.

When she has this time, she can take a more positive perspective toward her children.

My best example of showing love when you don't feel loving came from my daughter. At less than five years old she had a tremendous amount of empathy and insight. Once when she became very upset about having to transition from one activity to another, she shouted, "I don't love—" At that point, I tensed up and braced myself. I just knew she was going to tell me she didn't love *me*, and I knew it would hurt. Instead, she paused, took a deep breath, and finished her sentence. "I don't love . . . how you take away fun!" I was relieved on the inside and had to hold back a smile. Even at the tender age of five, my daughter was able to demonstrate love even when she was angry and did not feel loving. She showed self-control when she wanted to lash out. She knew what she was about to say wasn't the truth, and she didn't want to hurt my feelings by saying she didn't love me. And we both knew that was far from reality.

When our son was a few weeks old, we took him to the pediatrician for his checkup. The doctor, herself pregnant, made a joke about how sometimes, even when parents love their babies, it can take some time to *like* them. After all, taking care of newborns is exhausting work. With our son, this involved enduring nearly incessant crying. That can be hard to take! It resulted in my feeling anxious and helpless, unsure if I would ever be able to comfort this tiny, but loud, human. We always loved him, even when we didn't feel the love in the moment. And we certainly didn't know if he would ever love us. Regardless of our momentary feelings, we always want our children to know they are loved. So, how else can parents show love even when they don't feel it? Read on for some more insights on grace.

EXTEND GRACE

As we get into the meat of the five love languages and their application to adoptive families, we'll share lots of examples of how to demonstrate love. Many of those ideas can be put into action even when we don't feel loving toward our children. After all, it's tough to feel loving toward a child who is being disrespectful, disobedient, or destructive toward us or others. Yet sometimes, those moments are the exact times to show our love. I recall a time when I was standing behind my daughter as she was at the bathroom sink getting ready for bed (well, she was supposed to be getting ready for bed). We could both see ourselves in the mirror, and my daughter caught sight of the change in my facial expression and body language as I was getting frustrated with her negative behavior. All of a sudden, the Lord moved my heart and I totally relaxed. My little girl noticed and said, "Mama, that was a whole lot of grace right there!" Oh, that melted my heart and is a story that replays in my mind when I'm tempted to get upset, especially about trivial matters. Extending grace is one way we can show our children we love them, even if we don't feel the love. Another benefit is that it teaches them how to extend grace in return!

It's also important for parents who have adopted to extend grace toward themselves when, for instance, you feel unloving toward your child or you mess up, which all parents do sometimes. Abuse and neglect are never acceptable, but making mistakes is a common part of parenting.

We may place more pressure on ourselves because we know our children have been through painful life experiences and we don't want to cause any more pain. It's common for adoptive parents to go to extreme lengths to try to make up for what their child has been through or to make up for the time lost between the child's birth and the time the child came to live with their new family. This can be displayed in various ways, such as excessive permissiveness or an overabundance of material items. Yet, we're all imperfect and we cannot hold ourselves to the impossible standards of getting everything right 100 percent of the time. I like these words from Tim Kimmel: "If they're forming a line for parents who have fallen short, and you feel that you should be in it, you'll have to get in line behind me. We've all fallen short."[6]

None of us is going to parent perfectly, and the pressure to do so will result in disappointment and discouragement. I admit I am too hard on myself. Why don't we, together, commit to releasing the guilt and focusing on doing what we can while accepting our limitations?

LOVING ADOPTED CHILDREN
AS MUCH AS BIOLOGICAL CHILDREN

Can adoptive parents love their adopted child as much as biological parents love their children? What about when a parent has children both by birth and by adoption—will the biological child be loved more? In *Adopted for Life*, Russell Moore addresses some of these questions and shares examples of comments he and his wife have had made to them after adopting two children and having two biological children (in that order).

Comments are often made to couples who have biological children first that they should not adopt. And couples who have adopted children first are told, "Now you'll have biological children." (Or if the Lord does bless parents with adopted children followed by biological children, the comment goes something like "That always happens!")[7]

In fact, that does not *always* happen. I certainly know couples for whom this did happen—some while they were in the adoption process. One couple chose not to adopt, and another couple went on to adopt twins! However, I know far more for whom biological children were not in God's plan. Emphatically yes, adoptive parents can love their adopted children as much as biological parents love their biological children! And this is possible when you are a parent of both adopted and biological children.

DISRUPTED ATTACHMENT

Every child placed for adoption has "experienced a disrupted attachment."[8] This is true even when the adoptive parent(s) take the newborn child straight home from the hospital. That reality doesn't change the fact that the baby has been removed from the parent he or she has been carried by. This loss should be acknowledged, but so too should the fact that secure attachment can be developed between non-biological individuals. The most obvious example of this outside of adoption is the connection between a man and a woman. While there are certainly unhealthy marriages, many consist of two people who, while flawed, have developed a secure attachment.

Attachment styles are not established in our DNA. Rather, they are based on lived experiences and developed in childhood as a result of a caregiving relationship. Yet even adults who have challenging childhoods can go on to have satisfying marriages and other relationships. Experiencing trauma in childhood, even in utero, can result in a disrupted attachment. An adoptive parent who takes the initiative and time to develop a healthy attachment with their new child is also helping to set the child up for healthy relationships with others, now and in the future. (Attachment will be covered in more depth in the next chapter.)

ADOPTION STORIES

Steve and Diane adopted a child after many years of infertility. Diane shared that she never wanted to think of her daughter as being "on loan." Rather, this child would be her baby. While she had a lot of questions about the birth family, she tried day by day to be the best mom she could be. She felt the weight of responsibility of raising a child that the biological mother placed with them. Yet, there was never a question about how much Diane and Steve loved this baby. About five years after the adoption, Diane unexpectedly discovered she was pregnant and nearly halfway through her pregnancy. This was so unexpected that the couple first suspected Diane might have a growth. Nevertheless, Steve and Diane were thrilled, and they loved their adopted daughter and their biological daughter equally. Diane encourages other parents in similar circumstances to "be a part of their [children's] lives as best you can, have fun, be there, try to say yes more than no, and teach them of Christ's love for them."

Sometimes, it is only because of the love that Jesus gives us that parents are able to love the children He gives them. Gina shared her story of adopting two children internationally and the challenge she's experienced: "To be heartfelt, heartbreakingly honest, one child is easy to raise and easy to love and one isn't. But I do my best." For Gina, loving the child who isn't easy—due to complex needs—means working with therapists, hiring tutors, and buying her something small every time she goes to the store (because this child responds to gifts). Gina also shared that God gave her and her husband this particular child when Gina was mature enough as a parent to manage the challenges she would face.

A SERIOUS LACK OF LOVE

There are times when a parent experiences a serious lack of love for an adopted child. Here, we don't mean a frustrated or stressed-out parent, but one who has serious negative thoughts and feelings toward their child. This is likely due to a lack of attachment between you and your child. It could also be due to prolonged periods of lack of sleep, experiencing the trauma of being physically or emotionally harmed by your child, or going through the tough grind of nonstop caregiving. Regardless of the reason, if you lack any joy in this adoption journey, please keep reading—but also please reach out for both professional help and possible respite care.

Attachment bonding is possible but takes time and patience. One recommendation is to consider going through a Trust-Based Relational Intervention (TBRI) Caregiver Training or Connection Study. According to Texas Christian University's Karyn Purvis Institute of Child Development, "TBRI is an attachment-based, trauma-informed intervention" that addresses physical and attachment needs as well as reducing "fear-based behaviors."[9] Online and in-person training is available to caregivers of vulnerable children. The resource section of this book includes a helpful website.

While no one can ever guarantee that you will find pleasure in your parenting, please know you are not alone and that God sees you and will keep His promise to never leave you or forsake you. Sometimes the only reward in raising a child is knowing you have answered His call to care for a child in need. There is a blessing in that!

RUTHIE AND JACK: A CASE STUDY

In the previous chapter, Ruthie and Jack were introduced. They brought their daughter, Marlene, home from the hospital three days after her birth, and yet there was a struggle to bond and connect with her. While they loved the idea of having a child and being parents, they struggled with feeling love for this specific child, who it seemed cried every moment she was awake and often throughout the sleeping hours too. The couple desperately wanted to comfort her and experience those cherished emotions toward her but felt guilty that this wasn't happening like they'd expected. On the advice of a counselor, whenever the guilt started to get to one or both of them, Ruthie and Jack would pray. Sometimes individually, sometimes together. Sometimes all they could get out was a simple prayer of "Lord, help." This was often during times of high stress when Marlene could not be consoled, and Mom and Dad were worn out from lack of sleep. Ruthie and Jack found that praying helped calm them down, as did talking with one another and hugging one another. To be sure, they spent a great deal of time hugging Marlene too!

They also spent time writing out truths, such as:

Marlene is a gift from God.
We love Marlene.
Marlene will not cry all the time forever.
We can get help.
God loves us all and will help us as a family.

Some of the steps this couple took sound really simple—and they are. Yet, they yielded a high return as they gave Ruthie and Jack the emotional strength to make it through the first year and a half of being parents. When Marlene was about eighteen months old, things started to change. The attachment bond grew between her and her parents, the family began to adjust, and Ruthie and Jack were better able to comfort their daughter. It was clear that mama, daddy, and daughter were growing closer in their love for one another. Ruthie and Jack worked hard to be persistent in their pursuit of a loving family relationship and often reminded themselves that love takes time.

4

Attachment and Reactions

FOR SOME PARENTS, attachment does not come easy. Gina shared how she and her husband adopted an ill child via an international adoption. This child had experienced deprivation during her first year of life and would turn herself around at bottle-feeding time so she couldn't see her new mother. For years she also physically fought her mother when it was bath time. There was an attachment issue, not at all caused by the child or her mother, but by circumstances including early childhood trauma and exposure to alcohol in utero. In this chapter, we'll look at attachment styles as well as the ramifications of trauma and exposure to alcohol. We'll then look at how a secure attachment can be developed, as well as some suggestions for parents raising children who have fetal alcohol spectrum disorder or reactive attachment disorders.

ATTACHMENT STYLES

There are four attachment styles. Three of these styles are insecure, and one is secure. The three insecure styles are anxious-preoccupied, dismissive-avoidant, and fearful-avoidant. Those who have anxious-preoccupied attachment look to others to complete them; those who are dismissive-avoidant emotionally distance themselves from others; and the fearful-avoidant stay concerned about getting too emotionally close *or* too emotionally far away from others.[1] I have previously written about attachment styles in my book *Relational Reset: Unlearning the Habits That Hold You Back*, in which I included the information below about secure attachment:

> Adults who have a secure attachment style were securely attached to their parents as children and successfully became independent from them. With their parents, and then with other people, they are connected, but free. In a relationship they feel safe with the other person and go to that person when distressed. They feel seen and heard by that person.[2]

Social worker Cindy Lee identifies four characteristics of secure attachment: proximity ("Do we like to be together?"); safe haven ("Do I return to my caregiver when I am sick or scared?"); secure base ("Do you have me so I can explore the world?"); and separation distress ("Do I experience some anxiety when we are apart?").[3] Children want to know they are safe, and that it's okay for them to go out (or even walk a short distance away from Mom), knowing the parent will be there when they come back.

Once again, it's crucial for parents to develop a secure attachment with a child who has been adopted, especially since 80 percent of children going into foster care have unresolved attachment.[4] Before discussing ways to increase secure attachment, let's look at what can happen when a child does not receive the care he or she needs and deserves.

TRAUMA AND THE BRAIN

The brain develops until a person is in their mid-twenties.[5] (Doesn't that make you sit up and think?) The brain is often thought of as being upstairs, downstairs, left and right. Harvard-trained psychiatrist Dr. Daniel J. Siegel has done significant research on the brain. He and coauthor Dr. Tina Bryson describe the left side of the brain as being *logical*, *literal*, *linguistic*, and *linear* and loving lists and the fact that all the first words in this list start with the same letter.[6] The right brain "cares about the big picture," sends and receives signals related to communication, and is "emotional, nonverbal, experiential, and autobiographical."[7] Not only does the brain have two hemispheres, but there are also upstairs and downstairs brains. The lower brain manages basic functions, impulses, and emotions, while the upper brain is more advanced.[8]

In order to function optimally, children have to be taught to integrate both hemispheres of their brain as well as the lower and upper brains. But remember how this section began with a startling fact about brain development and age? The upstairs brain is incomplete in any child, but for children who have experienced trauma—such as children who have been adopted—there are additional concerns, including the impact of fetal alcohol spectrum on the brain and reactive attachment disorder. Before we look at those, we'll explore the fight, flight, freeze, fawn, and flop responses that children may experience as a result of having undergone trauma—and how this may interfere with a parent and child securely attaching.

Fight, Flight, Freeze, Fawn, Flop

Let's begin with the last one in this list of fight, flight, freeze, fawn, and flop. Flop may be one you haven't heard of. The study of stress reactions first identified fight-versus-flight reactions, and the other reactions have been added as more research has been conducted. The flop reaction is a more recent concept. Basically, this is a more severe form of freezing.[9] When someone who has experienced trauma freezes in response, they are often numb or shut down.[10]

The phenomenon of fight versus flight has been documented in the literature since the 1920s,[11] with the freeze response identified starting in the 1950s.[12] These stress reactions have primarily been based on animal studies; however, we know that human beings are a bit more complex. Nevertheless, there are at least five reactions that have been identified, if not more. The fight reaction occurs in those who "become combative or overly defensive," whereas the flight reaction is when those who have experienced trauma "abruptly remove themselves from the situation."[13] One of my children falls into the latter category. Sometimes at the mere hint of something not going this child's way, the reaction is to run.

My sister, who worked for many years in preschools, has shared about children who are deemed *runners*. This is the child you must keep an eye on at all times lest they dart out of the door and into the parking lot. That tendency in young children is related to the brain, but for a child who has been traumatized, it can remain after the age at which most other children have grown out of this tendency. The child simply must get away from the situation, attempting to outrun even emotional distress. Oh, how I can relate! On a number of occasions after the death of a close loved one, I *felt* like running away. And I don't mean I wanted to lace up my sneakers and go for a jog—though that can be a healthy coping skill. For the child who takes flight, running away is the best way their brain knows to try to escape.

For children who do not resort to flight, who do not fight, and who do not freeze or, worse, flop, they may experience a fawn reaction to trauma. In this case, there is movement toward the source of the trauma. This is common for victims of child abuse.[14] This can look like being submissive or agreeable. Just as we don't want our children to constantly live in a state of fight, flight, or freeze, we also shouldn't want them to automatically seek to please others, fear saying no, avoid conflict, or overly rely on others. It's particularly troublesome that later in life, according to trauma research, this reaction "can manifest as being highly submissive, looking to others to shape your reactions and relationships and struggling to make sense of yourself or your daily life on your own."[15]

The fawn reaction is similar to what has been identified as self-change behavior, which can happen when a physically abused child seeks to adjust to survive and make sense of their experience.[16] Heartbreaking! When we think about the fact that our children have suffered in some way or another, and we strive to put ourselves in their shoes, our empathy should allow us to better understand why our children may fight us, run away from us, seemingly freeze, or even fawn over us or other adults. Our sweet children need so much love—even when they don't seem sweet and even when we don't feel loving!

Fetal Alcohol Spectrum Disorders

The negative impact of alcohol on a developing baby's brain cannot be overstated. Because about 70 percent of children involved with the foster care system have been prenatally exposed to alcohol, the majority of children with fetal alcohol spectrum disorders (FASD) are not being raised by their biological parents.[17] Rather, they are being raised in foster and adoptive homes. Perhaps with parents like you. The symptoms of FASD listed below may be all too familiar to you, but a child on this spectrum could exhibit any of the following:

- low body weight
- poor coordination
- hyperactivity
- difficulty with attention
- poor memory
- difficulty in school
- learning disabilities
- speech delays
- low IQ
- sleep problems as a baby
- vision or hearing problems
- heart, kidney, or bone problems
- small head size
- abnormal facial features[18]

Despite there being no cure for FASD, there are a number of protective factors, including an early diagnosis (prior to age six), receiving appropriate services, and a loving, nurturing, and stable home environment.[19] Those last seven words should give you hope. If you have adopted a child with FASD or believe your child may be showing symptoms, the fact that you are providing a loving, nurturing, and stable home environment can help your child reach their "full potential."[20] If you have not done so already, please seek help through your child's physician. There may also be resources available through early intervention programs or public school systems.

Reactive Attachment Disorder

The American Psychiatric Association publishes a diagnostic and statistical manual of mental disorders, which mental health professionals use to diagnose individuals with mental, emotional, and/or behavioral health issues. One of the categories is Trauma- and Stressor-Related Disorders. This section contains diagnoses that are specifically related to an individual having been exposed "to a traumatic or stressful event."[21] A child who comes to your family via adoption did not ask or desire to experience a break in the connection between biological family and child. Yet, as a result of that experience, challenging emotions and/or behaviors can emerge.

In cases where there is insufficient care, a child might develop reactive attachment disorder (RAD). Some symptoms include not seeking comfort or not responding to comfort despite being distressed, limited positive moods, and "episodes of unexplained irritability, sadness, or fearfulness that are evident even during nonthreatening interactions with adult caregivers."[22]

DEVELOPING SECURE ATTACHMENT

Attachment disorder symptoms such as those we just noted can sound scary and be challenging, but there is hope. Fortunately, there are a variety of ways that attachment can be developed. For example, parents can co-regulate with an emotionally dysregulated child, who can then learn how to self-regulate. That's a mouthful! Perhaps an example would help. Secure attachment is rooted in safety and security.[23] Let's say a three-year-old accidentally gets a little scratch while playing with another child and begins to cry. If his mother immediately goes to the child, picks him up, and says soothing (truthful) words to him, such as "I'm so sorry you were hurt. Your boo-boo is a little red, but it will be okay," the next time the child is injured, he will know he can turn to his mother for comfort and receive just what he needs to emotionally feel better. Time and time again he can do this, as long as is necessary, until the point he is able to tell himself, "This hurts a little, but it will be okay." The child is then securely attached enough to seek his mother when he is hurt—and to know his mother will respond to his pain—but also secure enough to become independent as appropriate.

One helpful way to think through secure attachment is through the Circle of Security, which is a "visual map of attachment."[24] Circle of Security International (COSI) states that parents typically raise their children based on their own past experience, the advice of others, and their own beliefs about the best way to parent. While many are looking for the next-best parenting solution, decades of attachment research demonstrate that relational interventions (rather than behavioral interventions) create lasting security.

The circle of security consists of three parts: going out, coming in, and hands on. Using this model, we can identify the three needs children have that correspond to each of the three parts. The first need is the freedom and confidence to **go out** and explore the world, knowing their parents will encourage them, delight in them, and be ready to enter new adventures with them. The second need is knowing that, when they are ready, the child can **come back** to the parent for comfort and protection and that the parent will refill their emotional cup, be delighted to welcome them back, and understand them. Finally, children need caregivers to be **hands on** and in charge in a kind way, exhibiting strength, availability, and the ability to identify needs. In order for secure attachment to develop, children cannot be held too close when they need to go out or kept at a distance when they need emotional support. They need to know their parents can be trusted when the child is lost, confused, or even out of control.

While this is a relational rather than a behavioral approach, children who are more secure behave better when treated in this manner. The emotional connection between parent and child matters.

The reality is that children who come from hard places (a phrase coined by Karyn Purvis)—foster care in particular—"have intermittent emotional bonds with caregivers which may affect development of attachment styles."[25] For the parent who has adopted, working to increase the secure attachment can be a big task, but not an insurmountable one. There is research to indicate that the secure attachment to the parents—specifically the mother but also the father—has a positive impact on the child. One example is for a parent to be "flexible in recognizing and regulating emotions."[26] If the parent is not able to do this, it will be a challenge for that parent to teach their child how to recognize and regulate their own emotions.

Secondly, personal counseling for the parents who have adopted can be critical in making progress on secure attachment. Counseling is helpful not only for the parent and child, but also for the parents (separate or together) as they work through their own attachment issues that might be barriers to forming a closer relationship with their children.

In addition to being responsive to a child's needs and helping him or her recognize and regulate emotions, as well as working on your own secure attachment to others, a third way to build a secure attachment with a child who has been adopted is through understanding and applying the five love languages we are going to cover in the next five chapters.

While much of what you have just read about attachment may include academic terms with which you are unfamiliar, it's important to recognize that building a healthy emotional attachment with your adopted child is valuable to both you and your child. With adopted children, this process will take time for the reasons noted in this chapter. However, we believe that understanding the five love languages can help parents build a healthy emotional bond with their adopted child.

As I (Gary) indicated in the introduction of this book, one of a child's deepest emotional needs is to feel loved by the significant people in their lives. No one is more significant in the life of an adopted child than their adoptive parents. What you are about to read in the next five chapters are five ways to express love on the emotional level: the five love languages. Learning to speak these languages on a consistent basis will greatly enhance the parent's ability to effectively meet the child's need for love.

I like to picture, inside every child, an emotional "love tank" waiting to be filled. When the love tank is filled, the child feels safe and connected to the person who is expressing love. When the tank is running on empty, the child will feel distant and untrusting. Much of the misbehavior of children grows out of an empty love tank.

The key is understanding that each child has a primary love language; one of the five will speak more deeply to them emotionally than the other four. So, discovering the child's primary love language and "speaking" it to them regularly is essential. Then, as noted earlier, we want to learn and speak the other four languages as well. The goal is that the child will learn how to receive and, in time, how to speak all five languages. This is preparing them to have loving relationships throughout life.

5

Acts of Service

WHEN I WAS A LITTLE GIRL, I had pet rabbits. Our family had a menagerie of animals—dogs, cats, birds, hamsters—but the rabbits were my favorite, and they were all mine. Only one at a time was allowed, and my first little rabbit had white fur and pink inside her ears. My daddy built a cage with wheels for her, so I could push her around our yard. I loved that little rabbit and always tried to take good care of her. One day it was pouring rain, and I wanted to go out and check on her. I put on my little yellow raincoat and made my way into the mushy backyard to discover my sweet rabbit covered in mud and lying dead not far from our house. My seven-year-old heart was broken, and I went running back in the house crying. Because my dad was at work, my brother Jake went out and buried my beloved pet for me. Despite the fact that he was five years older than I, and we didn't have much in common at the time, his burying my bunny in the rain demonstrated his love for me. I'll never forget that kind act of service. Acts of Service is a powerful love language! Let's look at how this plays out in adoptive families.

ACTS OF SERVICE AND ADOPTED CHILDREN

Every child has basic needs that can only be met through acts of service. As children age, they can contribute to meeting these needs, but they all start out needing others to feed them, bathe them, and change their diapers and clothes. They need their laundry washed; they need care when they are sick; and they need transportation wherever they must go. Sometimes, even when a child *can* do something for themselves, they want the caregiver to do it for them. This could mean the child simply doesn't want to do it, and the parents have to encourage and motivate them to do it. On the other hand, this could mean a child emotionally needs that act carried out by the parent to help them feel loved, connected, wanted, or cared for. If these acts seem to be significant to a child, that might be a sign that this is their primary love language.

The acts of service we provide for our children should be differentiated from the tasks we do for them out of necessity. My daughter still needs help unbuttoning the top button on the back of her dresses. While this is an act of service, unbuttoning that button is not really about showing her love. However, when my very capable little girl asks Mama or Daddy to help her put on her socks and shoes, she is seeking special attention. She has shared with us that while she can put these on herself (which we are well aware of), she enjoys having this help. I don't mind doing this, and I know that one day she'll stop asking for help in this way. I hope these moments—her sitting on the loveseat and me sitting on the stool in front of her as I pull up her socks and lace her shoes—will be remembered as sweetly by her as they are by me. Although my son can walk (and run!), he likes being carried. Not only does this provide physical contact and relieve his little legs, but this is an act of service that shows him Mama and Daddy care about him. I know that he, like his sister, won't always ask for help in this way, so as often and as long as my body will allow me to do so, I hoist my big baby onto my hip and give him a ride.

For children who have been adopted—especially those who were with another family before yours—some acts of service have to be prolonged. It could be that the child never learned properly in a prior household. For example, you might expect a child to be able to take care of his or her toileting needs properly by a certain age, but if this need wasn't adequately attended to previously, you may need to continue helping a child with this long after most children that age might require help. Or it could be that the child simply needs to "revert" to a baby-like stage in order to work toward better attachment with you. Even as a kindergartner, my daughter liked for me to occasionally take a spoonful of food and pretend like I was zooming an airplane through the air or chug-chug-chugging a train into her mouth. Feeding her, even though she can feed herself, is an act of service that helps with our bond. Another thing my children have benefited from is being rocked—well into their preschool and elementary years. The neat thing about this act is that it also encompasses other love languages such as Physical Touch, Quality Time, and often Words of Affirmation, as I softly whisper sweet words to them as we rock back and forth. Actions have consequences, and these tender moments are one meaningful way to demonstrate love, resulting in a calmer, happier, better adjusted, and more attached child.

Like many young children, Alexis did not like cleaning up. Her mother tried everything. She tried singing, "Clean up, clean up, everybody everywhere. Clean up, clean up, everybody do your share!" (Now that song is stuck in your head—you're welcome!) While Alexis would sing along with her mother, she wouldn't clean up. Then her mom tried to make it a game to see how fast Alexis could clean up her mess. That didn't work either. She even threatened to take away whatever toys and dress-up clothes were not picked up; Alexis wouldn't budge.

Then her mom had an idea. She offered to help Alexis clean up. "Alexis, what if we do this together? I will help you, if you will clean up with me." Alexis's eyes lit up as she readily agreed. Her mom was providing an act of service by cleaning up a mess she had not made. This step demonstrated to Alexis that her mom wasn't solely trying to have power and control over her (a big deal for many kids, especially those who have been adopted), but that she was willing to help her. This act also reminded Alexis that her mom loved her and cared for her, confirmation that Alexis was constantly seeking. I'm not suggesting that all children everywhere get out of cleaning up by themselves for all time. Not at all. Of course, parents want children to become independent and to become capable of taking care of themselves. But in this particular instance, the burden Alexis felt was lightened, and the relationship she had with her mother benefited from this act of service as their attachment grew. The house benefited too! In time, Alexis started to clean up her mess more and more on her own, and now she has no problem cleaning up when Mom asks her to do so.

ACTS OF SERVICE AREN'T ALWAYS EASY

We know that acts of service aren't always easy. Parenting often involves wiping bottoms, cleaning up vomit, and taking care of injuries. And it's not always fun to complete chores for others, even when you love them and they feel loved because of your actions. But those aren't the routine acts I'm referring to. In this section, we want to address diving deep into a child's history and adoption story as an act of service. For far too long, adoptions were a big secret, kept from everyone including the adoptee. A friend of mine didn't discover she was adopted until she was a teenager. What a shock! While not all experts agree on an exact age, many experts agree on weaving the adoption story into the child's life from the start. In fact, there doesn't ever have to be a moment when they remember learning for the first time that they were adopted.

A great way to talk about adoption is through the use of books written for children to help educate them in age-appropriate ways about their stories. Some book suggestions are included in the resource list at the end of this book. Yet just because a child has "always" known they are adopted, that doesn't make getting into the details of the adoption easy. The details must be shared in age- and developmentally appropriate ways. Some details are too heavy a burden for a young child to carry. However, it's always important for a child to hear the truth, including the truth that they are loved. As children get older, they will sometimes want to know more details about their background. One adoptive mother I know took one of her teenage children on a drive past his first home in another state after he asked her numerous times if they could do so. She did all she could to emotionally prepare him (and herself), but it was still a painful journey to take. While not a typical act of service, this was certainly a movement of kindness. Sometimes the actions we take for our children aren't easy, and sometimes there is emotional risk involved. At the same time, these actions go a long way in demonstrating the love we have for our children.

When parents go above and beyond for their children, they are demonstrating the important value of helping others. Many people are familiar with the Golden Rule, but not as many are aware that this is actually found in the Bible: "So in everything, do to others what you would have them do to you" (Matthew 7:12). There is plenty of research that supports the notion that in helping others, we help ourselves. People feel better when they look beyond themselves and their own circumstances and do something for others.

I can personally attest to this with many examples, but one sticks out. During the ups and downs of the COVID pandemic, there was an increased need for Meals on Wheels drivers. Meals on Wheels is an organization that delivers meals to homebound people, predominantly senior citizens, who are incapable of meal preparation. Despite the stressors I was personally experiencing, I decided to go through the training and make some deliveries. I took my daughter on a number of occasions, and doing so helped me get beyond myself and my own struggles. It also demonstrated to my daughter the importance of serving others and helped her learn how to provide acts of service to those in need.

Teaching our children about serving others should be regularly integrated into our lives. It shouldn't just be about volunteering at the homeless shelter on Thanksgiving, but about making serving others a part of who we are. Jesus didn't come to be served, but to serve.[1] We should do the same and model this lifestyle for our children.

BACK TO RUTHIE AND JACK

Let's take another look at Ruthie and Jack. With Marlene being so young, they naturally performed many acts of service for her. Remember how we said that these necessary acts that all caregivers should provide need to be differentiated from the demonstration of love through acts of service? While that is true, one thing to keep in mind is *how* the love is demonstrated through an act of service. For example, Marlene started coming home from preschool with half of her lunch uneaten and a grumpy attitude (in part due to hunger) about what her mom was packing for her. "Mama, you know I don't like green beans! Why do you keep putting those in my lunch?" While Ruthie's goal was to pack a nutritious and well-balanced lunch for Marlene to take to preschool each day, Ruthie began to make sure to include the healthy items she knew her daughter loved, so that her daughter would open her lunch box and exclaim, "Yummy!" and enjoy her lunch. Ruthie also started to put in notes with simple drawings or words that her daughter would know meant she was loved and thought of while they were apart.

In the mornings, Jack usually helps get Marlene up and ready for the day. He knew Marlene didn't like to be rushed out of bed only to have to make her bed and immediately get dressed for the day. They had battled over that for a while before it occurred to Jack that instead of expecting his child to change, he could make some changes himself to help. So, he began to get up early, go into his daughter's room and sit on the side of her bed, rub her back (Physical Touch!), and gently let her know that he would be back in about fifteen minutes to help her get up. Although she was capable of putting on her own clothes and even making her bed, Jack always helped her because he knew that this morning time was an opportunity to demonstrate the care he had for his little girl.

A FINAL THOUGHT

If you are having trouble getting your adopted child to do things that you know they are capable of doing, you might simply ask: "Would you like for me to help you do this?" If they say yes, you can be pretty sure that the love language of acts of service communicates love to them. This helps build the emotional bond with your child. I predict that the time will come when they will say, "I can do this by myself. I don't need your help anymore." (Welcome words to the parent's heart.)

Acts of service are meaningful to all children, but they speak deeply to the child whose primary love language is Acts of Service. The Scriptures admonish us to express our love not only in words, but by our actions (1 John 3:18).

6

Gifts

WE HAD NOT BEEN LIVING in our new house very long when I took my daughter along as I browsed estate sales for just the right pieces of furniture to complete my home decorating. We arrived at one older home, and my little girl was delighted to find a room full of porcelain dolls and accessories. We had a ball sorting through them, and I was especially thrilled to find one that was identical to a doll I had as a little girl. My sweet daughter and I sat there and were carefully rocking those dolls when she discovered one that came in its own wooden carrying case, lined with satin. The doll could be secured with ribbons to prevent it from being jostled around and broken, and it even had an extra outfit on a hanger.

My daughter loved the doll and begged me for this treasure. Upon finding out the fairly low cost (versus the actual value), I gave in and agreed to buy a porcelain doll for my kindergartner. I know what you're thinking. Not a smart move, Mama. And you'd be right. It was only a few days later when she confessed to me that she was making the doll clap her hands and had broken them in the process. There was no fixing this doll, and she had to be thrown away. Not only did I learn my lesson about purchasing breakable items for children who are too young to properly care for them, but a deeper realization occurred to me: Was it possible that I had agreed to that doll so that my daughter would feel loved in that moment? Was the need to say yes to her or to please her through this gift overriding my common sense and responsibility? Unfortunately, I think so.

When we talk about giving gifts as a love language, it's important for adoptive parents to be very cautious not to use gifts to overcompensate for what a child has lost or been through. Gift giving is a powerful and effective love language, when used appropriately. Using gifts in this way is the focus of this chapter. Using them inappropriately can set children up to become entitled or expect that they will always get what they want. While I want to say yes a lot to my children (and we should as often as we can), there are also times when the yes needs to be deferred. In the case of my daughter and the porcelain doll, I could have said, "Yes, honey, you may have a porcelain doll when you are older." I'll definitely try that next time! The reality is that no number of gifts will ever make up for what a child has lost by being apart from their biological family. Gifts are not intended to compensate for their pain, but rather offered as one avenue to show a great depth of love.

GIFTS AND ADOPTED CHILDREN

Some people are simply gift givers. My mama is one of those people. It is not at all uncommon to hear the chime on my Ring doorbell only to discover that an Amazon delivery driver has dropped off another package. She particularly enjoys purchasing clothing for the kids, but she has also been known to ask me for a child's school list and purchase just about everything on the list! One time, a sister asked Mama if she could help her find an item and made it clear she was not asking my mother to make the purchase for her. Within minutes, our super-sleuth mother had found and paid for the item. My reply? "Mama, I have been looking for a minivan." Unfortunately, that didn't work, but we all got a laugh out of it.

My sisters and I all received the gift-giving gene from our mother. One sister is more like a secret sister in that she has gifts delivered without signing her name and without any expectation of recognition or anything in return. Not everyone's primary love language is receiving gifts. For some folks, there are other ways they prefer to be shown love. Yet, all children need a gift from time to time, even when it's not their birthday or Christmas. When a child expectantly awaits presents and cherishes gifts given to them, you can know Gifts is their love language.

As I write this story, it is the fifth anniversary of the day we adopted our daughter. The day before the first anniversary of her adoption, my husband, Nick, went to the Build-A-Bear store (alone!) and made two stuffed animals for our girl. One was a fluffy white bear with a blue dress and crown, dressed like the princess we knew our sweet child to be. The other was a cocoa brown monkey holding a red heart. I was proud of Nick for his creations. After all, he had never purchased gifts like these before, and he had certainly never created them before! The next day, we took our "baby" into the living room and set her in the leather recliner. Her daddy held up her two gifts. She oohed and aahed over the princess and came to love the monkey in time. These are gifts we hope our daughter will cherish, as they were given to show our delight in her and absolute joy that she had joined our family.

While our daughter had been treated well by her first caregiver (an amazing woman biologically related to her, whom we also love), many children do not come into their new families with many possessions. It is not uncommon for children who have been in foster care to show up at the would-be adoptive family's home with only a trash bag's worth of belongings. No matter how many times we move and declutter, I won't ever have only one small bag of stuff. What these children have is important to them, and every item given can seem like a treasure. This is especially true when there is thought placed into the gift, and when it is accompanied by other expressions of love so that the children are ensured the gift is not compulsory or overcompensation.

I have learned to be very careful about throwing items away. When one of my children makes a piece of artwork for me, that is their way of showing love for me! It makes me think of the times my brother gave me a handmade birthday card. Since he passed away, I am even more grateful I kept these. While we can't keep everything we're ever given, we have to be mindful to both give and receive gifts graciously. Sometimes, that does not work out as planned.

GIFT REJECTING

On her ninth birthday, Olivia's parents went into her bedroom to wake her up and surprise her with balloons and flowers. A special dinner, followed by cake and presents, was planned for later. Much to their surprise, the little girl who had only been home with them for six months woke up grumpy and became upset with them over what they had planned. "I told you I didn't want anything for my birthday! Just leave me alone!" Her parents quietly left the room, sad and confused by what had just taken place . . . on what they had assumed would be a happy day for their new daughter.

What Olivia's parents failed to consider was how this special occasion might be a trigger for her. In fact, many days that most families consider special are particularly challenging for children who have been adopted, especially birthdays.[1] It's not uncommon for adoptive parents to witness a change in behavior on or near a birthday. These can include crying over small things, emotional distance, anger, sadness, and reluctance.[2] For Olivia, the balloons were a reminder of her birth family. Despite abuse perpetrated by her biological father and allowed by her biological mom, her birthday was the one day a year Olivia was shown kind attention and care. There were always balloons and cake at a party with her extended family to try to mask what was going on behind closed doors. It was the one day when Olivia felt loved by her first mother, and her birthday made her miss her and long for her. Olivia's new parents didn't know this. Their intention was to show her how happy they were to have her in their family and to demonstrate to her that her life was of great value and worth. Unfortunately, it didn't work out that way.

Adoptive parents have to be aware of potential triggers and also have a contingency plan for when the unexpected happens. In Olivia's case, her mom might have said something like, "Honey, I am so sorry that you are upset. Daddy will take the balloons and flowers downstairs, and we can decide what to do about the party later. For now, I'll just sit here with you and am available if you want a hug or to talk." With time and space, Olivia may come around to deciding she would like to create some new birthday memories with her new family. If she doesn't, a celebration shouldn't be forced, but birthdays will likely need to be a topic for future counseling sessions. Perhaps the best gift a parent can give the birthday girl or boy is "the gift of no expectations."[3]

GIFT IDEAS THAT MAY BE RIGHT FOR YOUR CHILD

Many moms purchase matching mommy-daughter outfits to wear for holidays and special occasions. This may be one way to give a gift to your daughter and demonstrate the similarities that the two of you can have, even though you are not biologically related. Another gift-giving option that is particularly powerful for transracial adoptees is to give a doll that looks like your child, or to give clothing, music, or even candy that pertains to your child's culture.

I know several big families with both biological and adopted children (three have eight children each!). It's not always possible to give a grandiose gift, but even giving small gifts can be a reminder that each child is loved. One young lady gleefully explained that her father would hide gifts around the house for them to find. Each child's name was attached to a gift, and in an effort to reduce the potential for sibling rivalry, the gifts were evenly distributed among the children.

I'll never forget this girl's story about how her daddy gave gifts in this way.

A GOOD EXAMPLE

In addition to the love that it demonstrates to our children, giving them gifts teaches them about the importance of selflessly giving to others. Research shows that there are emotional rewards to giving. One study among at-risk youth focused on the impact of spending money on others.[4] These youth experienced a greater positive emotional impact from buying something for someone in need than they did when purchasing something for themselves.

My husband and I give our older child an allowance. She donates 20 percent to church, she saves 20 percent, and she gets to keep 60 percent to spend how she chooses. She cheerfully pulls money out of her little unicorn wallet to take to church. This act of giving comes naturally to her because this is what she has been taught. There are many ways to teach this, but helping our children learn to give gifts of all kinds to others will help set them up for a lifetime of selfless behavior.

One church in our community collects gifts for the Department of Social Services to distribute to children in foster care. Many of our children were at one point on the receiving end, and giving back to others in need is another opportunity to use gift giving as a way of expressing love.

MARLENE AND GIFTS

While Olivia struggled with receiving gifts, Marlene (Jack and Ruthie's daughter) used to love receiving gifts. She would ooh and aah over the brightly wrapped packages and squeal excitedly as she carefully unwrapped a present. Her parents were surprised at how much care she took in the process and how grateful she was for each gift regardless of what it was. Then, things changed. Marlene no longer seemed to care about what she was given, and Ruthie and Jack feared Marlene was becoming ungrateful or entitled. Bringing this issue to their counselor, they were asked to give some more details about what had taken place.

"Well," Ruthie said, "it began soon after we brought home the baby. We had told Marlene the baby was a gift to our family, but she has struggled with having a sister."

As Ruthie began to reflect on what she had just shared, Jack spoke up. "It's as if gifts have taken on a different meaning for Marlene now. She is no longer excited about them because they could be something that disrupts her life even more . . . or that she'll have to share with the whole family."

The couple had a lightbulb moment and explored this further with the counselor. By the end of the session, they were prepared to return to Marlene and explore this with her, helping her to understand that while the new baby was there permanently and they would all work together to adjust as a family, Marlene would still receive gifts that were just for her. In fact, Ruthie began planning for a trip to a special store where Marlene could create a doll. Marlene was thrilled and the love of receiving gifts from her parents returned.

A FINAL THOUGHT

Keep in mind that we want to give gifts that will enrich the child's life, and we want to give gifts that are age appropriate, not porcelain dolls for a kindergartner. As parents, we must not allow a child's pleading to cause us to cave in and give them a gift we think is inappropriate. Doing so trains the child that all they have to do to get what they want is to get angry and upset. This will not serve them well as adults. The proper response to a child pleading with you for something might be: "Honey, I love you too much to give you that because I don't think it would be good for you." I know this is not always easy. When my little boy folds his hands under his chin, peers up at me with his big blue eyes, and sweetly says, "please," it's hard for me to say no. The child may not be happy with your saying no to the request, but they are learning an important lesson: we don't always get what we want when we want it.

Giving gifts as an expression of love is universal. The gifts need not be expensive. Remember the old saying: "It's the thought that counts." Also, one child may express greater excitement when receiving a gift than will another child. One couple who had two adopted daughters shared that when the husband was out of town on a business trip, he would buy identical gifts for each daughter. Once he bought two teddy bears (different colors). When he gave them to the girls, one was so excited, and said, "Thank you. Thank you. Thank you so much!" She hugged the bear, gave it a name, and called her grandmother to tell her. The other girl simply accepted the bear, tossed it on the couch, and asked her dad if he would show her the photos he'd made on his trip. The parents were concerned that she was not learning to express appreciation. After someone told them about the love languages, they realized that one daughter's primary love language was receiving Gifts and the other's was Quality Time. The daughter who tossed the bear aside before asking her dad about the pictures he took simply wanted her father's undivided attention.

7

Physical Touch

MY TWO-YEAR-OLD SON stepped on my toes. Literally. He would put his feet on top of mine, we would hold hands, and I would walk him across the room. He would howl with laughter the whole way. Seeing what fun we were having, my taller than average, almost six-year-old wanted in. She wanted the feet-to-feet and hand-to-hand contact, she wanted to be pranced across the floor, and she wanted to feel included. I mustered up my strength and gave it a whirl, never more thankful for the time I spent with my physical trainer. My kids loved this activity, and gleefully shouted, "Again! Again!"

Kids love playing with their parents, and that includes play with physical touch. I wouldn't be able to count the number of times I've heard "tickle me, Mama!" or "hold you, Mama!" I have carried on two kissing traditions that my father started when his five children were young. The first daily tradition was that he would place kisses in our hands that we could use anytime we were apart. While in school, I would often slip my hand up to my face and press a kiss from Daddy onto my cheek. In fact, I still do it from time to time.

The second tradition my daddy started—and I carry on with my children—was to kiss each cheek and forehead with a little saying that goes like this: "One for me. One for you. And one because I love you." I put kisses in my kids' hands in the morning, and give them kisses on their cheeks and forehead every night. I am thankful for the safe and gentle kisses I received from my father as a child and am thankful to pass that expression of love on to my children. In fact, on her own, my daughter started kissing me on my cheeks and forehead too. She changed the saying a bit to this: "One for me. One for you. And one because I love the whole family." Now my son asks for his kisses before nap time and bedtime: "I want my kisses!" He not only wants them, but he wants to give them. I cherish our time and our touch, as do my children, knowing that some of these sweet routines won't last forever. Thankfully, the memories will, and the physical touch they have and will experience from their daddy and me builds attachment, safety, and trust—and helps them feel loved. While "hugs and kisses are the most common way of speaking this love language," there are many ways that physical touch is used to demonstrate love.[1] Many children who thrive on physical touch will frequently touch their parents, ask to be held, or maybe ask for a back scratch.

Sadly, not all children have experienced safe physical touch. Some children come to our homes from prior environments where they experienced abuse or neglect. On one hand, they may not have ever experienced any physical touch, and on the other hand they may have experienced abusive touch in the form of physical or sexual abuse. It's heartbreaking to know this is the reality for some of our precious children. It can also make it difficult to connect physically with some children. After we talk about physical touch and adopted children, with some suggestions for touch (including when a child doesn't like to be touched or likes touch more than the parent does), we'll explore how to approach touch with children who have been abused.

PHYSICAL TOUCH AND ADOPTED CHILDREN

In an earlier chapter, I shared about Patricia and Ernie. One of the TBRI (Trust-Based Relational Intervention) healing strategies they teach is the effectiveness of soft, loving touch. Touch is critically important for the newborn child. Unfortunately, many children who have been adopted either did not receive enough safe touching from the start, or the caregiver changed from a biological mother to a foster or adoptive mother. Yet, it's not too late to use healing touch. As Ernie teaches, touch can stimulate the production of oxytocin, the love hormone, which promotes contentment and reduces anxiety and stress. It also stimulates the gland that regulates the body's production of white blood cells, which keeps us healthy. Finally, it stimulates the production of dopamine and serotonin, which can elevate mood and happiness. Ernie and Patricia teach that hugs should last over twenty seconds to have the most impact. Hug science proves this to be true, with research showing that hugs are healthy, cause a decrease in the release of cortisol, and can decrease both blood pressure and heart rate.[2]

In *Parenting the Hurt Child*, the adoption expert authors note that parents touch their children a great deal in the first few years of life, in particular as they feed and bathe them, and that we "constantly cuddle them for no reason whatsoever—except that we love them."[3] Because touch is important for secure attachment, it's important to touch children who have been adopted, even if they are older. Ernie and Patricia's touch suggestions include rubbing lotion on your children, scratching their backs, holding hands, cuddling, giving a foot rub, playing a hand-clapping game, giving a horsey ride, and giving a good night hug and kiss before bed.[4] There are many creative ways to provide healthy touch to children.[5] Another is to wash hands together. My daughter has always enjoyed washing her hands. She loves lathering on the soap and playing in the water. Sometimes when I remind her from another room that the water has been on for quite some time, she'll reply, "But I haven't even gotten the soap yet!" Yep, she loves being in the sink, and this was evident during a field trip I chaperoned at a farm. A gaggle of kids gathered around a large metal wash tub with a number of faucets running above it. Hanging down from the pipes were pantyhose with bars of soap tucked inside. The children would lather up their hands and then rinse off. My daughter was one of the last kindergartners to finish as she could not get enough of lathering up her hands. In fact, unlike me, she prefers bar soap to liquid hand soap. Yet, I stood there and washed my hands right alongside her, my hands on top of hers at times. She loves the sensation of soap—and she loves the sensation of being touched.

WHEN YOUR CHILD LOVES TOUCH—BUT YOU DON'T

There are times when a parent does not like giving or receiving touch nearly as much as his or her child does. In fact, some children are clingy to the point that it makes the parent uncomfortable. Yet not being engaged physically with the child could lead them to feel unloved or unwanted. This could trigger the thought that they could again experience separation from their parent. It certainly takes sacrificial love to show love via physical touch when this is not a parent's love language.

Kristen explained that this is her adopted daughter's love

language, but it is not hers. Her daughter loves to be held, have her back scratched, and sit as close as possible to her on the couch. Despite this not being Kristen's preferred method of demonstrating love, she engages with her daughter in these ways to ensure her daughter feels the love she has for her. Even swinging a child can allow for some physical touch—and quality time too!

When a child wants too much physical touch or is inappropriate in their requests or demands, setting boundaries is necessary. For example, if a child races outside to hug her mom just as she is unloading groceries from the car, Mom might reply, "I love you, and I want to give you a hug. Right now, my arms are busy. Once I put the groceries away, I'll not only give you a hug, I'll give you three hugs!" This reassures the child that you do want to engage in the physical touch, and you are still saying yes, but you are delaying this until the right time.

There may be times when a child plays too rough with other children when the real need is to receive physical input. If you see this happen, suggest that instead of playing rough, the child request games that involve gentle touch through play, such as patty-cake or ring-around-the-rosy. Yes, these old-fashioned games are still regularly played in my house! If a child is becoming too aggressive, the child should be separated from the other child (or children) until they calm down, but within view of the parent. This is often called a "time in" rather than a "time out."

During this time, there could be an opportunity for the parent to connect with the child via physical touch while also reminding the child of the need to be gentle with hands and body—and then encourage the children to reengage in a redo. We have done this as a whole family, resetting the stage as if we were going back in time to before the conflict took place. Everyone gets in place, and the child who needs to practice a better response then gets another chance. This helps reinforce what the child should do the next time. As the saying goes, "What fires together wires together."[6] This means that the more appropriate response, when repeated, can reinforce pathways in the brain that will hopefully result in the child returning to the appropriate response in the future.

WHEN TOUCH IS NOT SAFE OR WANTED

When a child has been physically abused or neglected, touch can be a challenge. Sometimes children from these backgrounds recoil from or rebuff physical touch. Because of their experiences or how their brains operate, they might perceive what could be a gentle touch as a threat. Sometimes children come into adoptive homes with a history of sexual abuse. Being aware of how this could impact the physical touch relationship between family members is important. While most children who have been sexually abused do *not* go on to sexually abuse others, understanding child sexual abuse (including signs and behaviors that may indicate a child has been sexually abused) is helpful to adoptive parents. Young children may imitate sexual acts with toys or stuffed animals; they may wet their bed or suck their thumbs; they may be curious about their bodies; or they may refuse to take off clothing at appropriate times or not have any inhibition about nudity.[7]

For these children, physical touch may seem scary as they perceive adults to be untrustworthy. Or a child may have unhealthy touch boundaries, and these should be clearly communicated.[8] Additionally, parents need to ensure that children are constantly supervised if there is any risk of your child touching other children. Everyone in the home needs to be respectful of every other family member's comfort level when it comes to touching, hugging, kissing, or tickling.[9] When a child does not wish to be touched, parents should move slowly rather than give up on this idea altogether (given all the evidence of its importance). Introduce touch carefully and gingerly. Do not pressure a child into something they do not want. Signs hanging at the entrances to amusement park rides warn that a scared child on the ground will panic in the air. Likewise, children who are already afraid to be touched may panic when actually being touched.

Another word of caution: children with sensory processing issues or disorders may perceive a threat that is not there. For example, if a child accidentally bumps them while waiting in the lunch line, the child who was bumped might react by coming out swinging. For all children, the rates of sensory processing disorder are about 15 percent, with rates believed to be higher for internationally adopted children.[10] Physical aggression is only one symptom of sensory processing disorder. If you have any concerns about this, an occupational therapist is the best person to contact for a full assessment. You may need a referral from your child's pediatrician.

MORE RESEARCH ON SAFE TOUCH

The literature on the benefits of healthy, safe touch with children is fascinating. Some of it makes great sense intuitively, but it's helpful to have the research to support what many parents already know. For example, one 2022 study of moms and preschoolers found that higher levels of positive touch were associated with lower levels of a stress reaction to a reminder of an upsetting experience.[11] This study contributes to the information already in existence on the importance of physical touch between parents and babies because it demonstrates the importance and benefits of continuing with physical touch beyond the first year of life. The physical maternal touch behaviors included hugging, kissing, snuggling, caressing, and holding. All things many kids love. I know my daughter does not want to leave for school without her kisses, and my son does not want to lie down for a nap or bed without his! I understand better now why these moments are especially beneficial.

One final research-related note. Going back to the love hormone formally known as oxytocin, there is evidence that multisensory context impacts functioning.[12] This means, in part, that for the touch to be beneficial to a child, the touch needs to be friendly and given with good intentions. This also means that touching a child gently with a scowl on your face will send mixed messages and will diminish the positive impact of the physical touch.

A GOOD EXAMPLE

When we use safe and gentle physical touch, we are teaching our children how to use this kind of touch with others. We are demonstrating what is acceptable and what is not acceptable. Based on Trust-Based Relational Interventions, when one of my children is not being kind with his or her hands, I remind them that people are not for hurting: hands are not for hitting people, legs are not for kicking people, etc. We can't teach children how *not* to be aggressive by being aggressive with them. And we can't teach them merely by telling them not to be aggressive. Writers are often told to "show, don't tell." The same is true for parenting. We must show our children how to use physical touch in healthy ways, rather than just tell them how to use it. We can't use the old adage "Do as I say and not as I do." They will recognize this as hypocritical behavior and resent us for it.

Children who have been adopted won't always come to us knowing about safe touch. They may have previously witnessed fighting or been forced to fight for self-protection. As their parents, we have to help them unlearn these behaviors, which takes a lot of attention on developing secure attachment and helping them to reduce the strong fight reaction that has become ingrained in their nervous system. We must be the good example they need in order to learn how to calmly resolve our conflict and discipline our children without resorting to harmful physical touch.

MORE ON MARLENE

Let's return to our case study of Jack, Ruthie, and Marlene. We learned in the last chapter that another baby girl has been welcomed into the family. This very likely impacted the way Marlene interacts with her parents. She used to love to be cuddled, but now sees the baby getting some of the time that was once hers. Instead of facing the possibility of feeling rejected (for example, her mother saying, "Sorry, sweetie, I am feeding the baby right now, so I can't hold you"), Marlene first rejects her parents when they reach out to her for hugs. This behavior has been clear to Jack and Ruthie, so they have started to incorporate physical touch in other ways.

An earlier example given was that Jack rubs Marlene's back in the morning. Another is that when Marlene is open to this, they have her sit on the couch and hold the baby. It's in those moments that she most feels like a big sister, and the glow of pride is on her face. Despite some initial protests, Marlene came around to allowing Ruthie to hold her and rock her like a baby. This physical touch helped reassure Marlene that even though she is not a baby, she is still loved just as much as she always has been and just as much as the baby. Ruthie and Jack also started to plan special time for each of them to spend with Marlene and also for the three of them to be together. (More on that in the next chapter on the love language of Quality Time.)

A FINAL THOUGHT

If you have adopted a child, don't assume you can immediately give them a hug, especially if they are older. They do not have an emotional bond with you yet. They may or may not have experienced an emotional bond with a former caregiver, and you are new in their lives. So, if they reject your attempt to hug them, don't be disturbed. (You would likely reject a hug from a stranger also.) It doesn't mean you can't touch them, but you must begin with a fist bump and later a pat on the back or a high five. As the emotional bond between the two of you begins to develop, eventually, they will be ready to receive your hugs.

8

Quality Time

I MENTIONED EARLIER that my husband was deployed while our son was a baby. It was a tough time for me. I was working full-time during a pandemic while caring for two children, depending on unreliable childcare, and trying to be there for my ill father. My daughter, three at the time, was having a tough time too. Who wouldn't? It became apparent that I needed some help to best parent her during those challenging months. In searching for some online resources, I discovered Positive Parenting Solutions.[1] One important suggestion the creator of the program offers is called "Mind, Body, and Soul Time." MBST "activities are spent one-on-one with each of your children, consistently and individually with each parent, doing an activity they choose." The idea is that this time will give parents a better bond with their children, but also that "the attention and power boosts will fuel better behavior."[2]

I was already spending a lot of time with my children—many days, every minute they were awake! But upon further exploration, I began to realize that the time together was not always quality time. And it certainly wasn't always centered on child's play that originated with what my daughter wanted to do. The time did not have to be long; even ten to twenty minutes a day was said to be beneficial. So, I began setting aside time for my daughter each night after the baby went to sleep that revolved solely around her and what she wanted to do. *Tea party?* Yes. *Let's pretend my bed is a boat and we have to go buy pickles?* Sure. *I'll be the cat owner and you'll be the cat, okay?* Alrighty then. No matter what, we had what we termed our "bestie time." Not only was this never taken away for poor behavior, but undesirable behavior was often an indicator that we needed to spend more time together—just the two of us. When my husband returned from deployment, he began a similar routine, dubbed "daddy-daughter time," or "DD time." We hope to continue this with our children into adulthood. Why? Because quality time is that important.

QUALITY TIME AND ADOPTED CHILDREN

Quality Time is "all about giving the other person your undivided attention."[3] For some, this is what they need in order to feel loved. How do you know if a child's love language is Quality Time? This child will frequently want to spend time alone with you, doing what they would like to do. There are many ways that parents can spend quality time with their children. With our busy lives and schedules, making time can be challenging. Yet, it should be a priority. In our home, the children make it clear when they need or want my attention. Picking up my phone or computer is a surefire way to ensure they will need me right then, regardless of what they were doing beforehand.

Shortly before he turned three years old, my son and I were home alone. He was quietly playing with magnets on the floor (quietly playing was a rarity!), when I decided to pull out my small laptop to try to get some work done. As soon as I opened my computer, my son came over to me and said, "I want to sit on your lap." Of course, I immediately closed my MacBook, and he climbed up for a cuddle. Some parents might say, "Son, keep playing with your magnets. Mommy needs to do some work." There are times when I have done that too. Yet, in that moment, it occurred to me that the communication my son received prior to my pulling out my computer was that I was available. He may not have needed me at that exact moment, but if the need should arise, I was right there for him. When I redirected my focus from him to my screen, all bets were off. To him, this was a sign that I might not be accessible, and this simply would not work for him. Hence, his request to sit with me.

Of course, this is common for young children. What is different for children who have been adopted is the interpretation of the metacommunication, which can be defined as the covert or underlying message.[4] Imagine this scenario: I pull out my computer, and my son asks to sit in my lap. I sigh with frustration and roll my eyes before finally saying, "Fine. Come on." Even a little one would receive the message that the request was an inconvenience. A child who is already sensitive about their place in the family might view it as something more than that. Even when a child is too young to really process or verbalize rejection, that feeling could become implanted within them. So, demonstrating that you have the time for them and that you want to make the time for them is crucial to their development.

Susan and Ashley never doubted their parents' love for them. Growing up, even with the parents' busy work schedules, they would go on an annual family trip to a cabin where their parents doted on them. At home, time together was more limited, but when they were all together, the parents focused on the girls. Now as adults, when the girls contact their mom and dad about visiting, their retired parents clear their schedule and invite their daughter(s) to stay as long as they'd like. Even after one of the girls had met her biological mother and started to spend time with her as well, these parents never stopped showing love to their children, nor did they ever question the love their children had for them. In fact, they viewed this as the family growing, rather than splitting apart. The family attributes the quality time the parents intentionally invested in their daughters as being a primary reason for the quality of the relationship today, some four decades after the girls were adopted.

A GUILT TRIP

Don't worry, you won't receive any guilt heaped on you from us! If you're like most parents, you already experience enough of that unwarranted feeling. I have certainly experienced my share. There are times I've thought that I should spend *all* of my time with my children and feel guilty when I can't or don't. Of course, many who mother their biological kids struggle with guilt, but I dare say there is something different about parenting children who have come to you through adoption. There is this sense that the child has already gone through so much, and that the only way for a secure attachment to develop is to spend 100 percent of your time together. While quality time is extremely important, this should not be used to compensate for a child's loss or assuage a parent's guilt. Children are smart, and they will pick up on whether you want to be with them. Instead of feeling guilty over the time you can't spend with your kids, invest in the time you are with them. We should put down our phones, turn off the television, and get off our couches. We should get on the floor with our kids to play, run around with them outside, and cuddle up with them to read books.

One of Gina's daughters plays golf, and Gina caddies for her. She says that they get four hours of "truly fun" time together each time her daughter plays a round. Cindy's kids love the beach, and she takes her crew as often as she can. They have made many wonderful memories during this quality time. Becky has a child who is a competitive gymnast, and Becky doesn't miss a meet. They travel to and from the out-of-state competitions, which allows them hours to chat and catch up on life. It's good for both of them. All the children in these families were adopted from hard situations. Their parents investing time in them reveals to these kiddos that they are truly loved.

BALANCING TIME

Early in our adoption process, my husband and I met with an adoption agency where the case worker explained that women who are planning to place their newborn for adoption sometimes want the adoptive mother to be a stay-at-home mom. She shared this with us to alert us that we might not be selected because I worked full-time. She went on to explain that biological moms don't always like the idea of relinquishing their child to a woman who is not going to raise the child full-time. While I have had a flexible job for many years (at this point, twice as long as I have been a mother), my children have attended a variety of preschool programs, mostly part-time in churches. But not all parents have this luxury, including devoted adoptive parents. Sometimes both parents are working traditional full-time hours out of financial necessity (and/or out of their calling from the Lord).

Of course, a woman choosing to place her child for adoption

has every right to make this decision, and I respect that. What I am suggesting is that it is important that we spend as much quality time with our children as possible. What many of these women had relayed to that adoption agency case worker makes a great deal of sense. And a little bit of empathy for your child can go a long way here. Imagine yourself in your child's shoes. You were either placed by your biological mother or removed from your birth parents. How would you feel if you then went into a home with parents who claim they love you, maybe even take care of your physical needs, but don't ever have any time for you?

One author shared about a boy who said his father cared about his hunting dogs more than him.[5] The evidence was the fact that when his dad arrived home each night, he made a beeline to the dogs. The boy's dad also brought the dogs treats and spent time with them on weekends. He never spoke harshly to his dogs but was critical of his son. When I put myself in the place of that child, I feel sad. I know if I were that kid, I would feel unwanted, uncared for, and certainly unloved. If only that father used the five love languages to show love for his child, starting with Quality Time. While a working parent and an unloving parent are certainly not equivalent, the point here is that we should always invest in time with our children—and not just being physically present in the same space but actually being involved with our children in a worthwhile manner.

A GOOD EXAMPLE

In Matthew 6, Jesus speaks about treasures in heaven versus treasures on earth. He tells His listeners that they should not store up things that can be destroyed or stolen. Instead, all of us should store up treasures in heaven, which can never be destroyed or stolen. He concludes by saying, "For where your treasure is, there your heart will be also."[6] When we invest in quality time with our children, we are showing them their value and we are teaching them the value of other people. We have an opportunity to show them the love of Jesus Christ, and they in turn can show that to others.

I recall a time when I had a friend in need. I took my daughter along to drop something off for this loved one. My daughter and I had some quality time in the car on the ride there, she witnessed my act of service in driving across town to my friend, she witnessed the gift that I passed along and the physical touch between my friend and me as we hugged, and she heard the affirming words I spoke over my friend. As we were driving away, an ambulance zoomed past us. My daughter immediately said, "Mama, there is someone hurt, and we need to pray now!" And we did. I believe that my child is becoming sensitive to others and their needs because not only am I sensitive to her needs, but I am mindful of the needs of others, and I model how to be present with and for those who are hurting.

Whatever we invest the most time in is what we truly care about. Please don't hear what I am *not* saying. I'm not suggesting that the mom or dad who is working two jobs and sixty hours a week to pay the rent and put food on the table doesn't care about their kids. The hard work proves they do care. Yet, as much as possible, we must invest quality time with our children so that they are assured and reassured over and over that they are loved and cared for—that we cherish them above our friends, above our activities, and above our technology. *Quality* time is more important than *quantity* time, but we cannot truly have the quality without the time.

THE IMPORTANCE OF QUALITY TIME

The case study in the last chapter—physical touch—ended with the note that Ruthie and Jack began having special time alone with Marlene. They knew it was important to their daughter, who craved time one-on-one with each of them and also time when the three of them were together without the baby—like it was before the new addition joined their family. While time as a family of four is also important and a priority for Ruthie and Jack, they have found Marlene to be much more secure when they each spend at least ten minutes a day alone with her. This quality time, without any distractions, reassures Marlene that she is loved and has an important place in the family. This time also helps to alleviate the thoughts that Marlene has that the baby is replacing her. Quantity time is important as children need a significant amount of time with their caregivers, but regardless of how much time is spent, ensuring that it is focused on the child at hand demonstrates that they are worth the time invested in them.

A FINAL THOUGHT

As we have illustrated in this chapter, quality time is giving the child your undivided attention. When having a conversation with your child, don't multitask. This means maintaining eye contact as much as possible and asking questions so that the child sees you're interested in their thoughts and feelings. Express understanding of their ideas and emotions by saying something like, "I think I am understanding what you're saying, and I can see how you would feel disappointed." Quality time also means doing things together: playing age-appropriate games with the child, taking walks together, doing an art project with them. Spending quality time demonstrates that you value the child; you enjoy being with them. Quality time is important for all children, but it speaks even more deeply to the child for whom this is their primary love language. If your child asks to spend more time with you or seems to liven up when you spend time with them, you'll know their primary love language might be Quality Time.

9

Words of Affirmation

IT'S OFTEN SAID that actions speak louder than words. But sometimes positive words are what are really needed to demonstrate that the motivation behind the actions is love. How do you know if a child's love language is Words of Affirmation? Note how the child responds to praise. If their little face lights up, that will be a sign. Offering words of affirmation doesn't mean exaggerating to puff up your child's ego. Rather, you speak truthful and positive words to them about who they are, like "you're brave," "you're kind to others," "you work hard." This is important for all children, but perhaps even more so for children who come from hard places. These children may have heard negative words spoken over them and about them in the past—and, sadly, "negative" may be an understatement. Even children who didn't have this experience can have doubts about who they are, about their worth, and about their value. Words of affirmation can make a tremendous difference in the lives of our children.

WORDS OF AFFIRMATION AND ADOPTED CHILDREN

I have often told my daughter that she is beautiful inside and out. One time she replied, "And the inside is most important!" I was so proud of my little girl for remembering this, and I hope she always takes that to heart. While there is nothing wrong with telling a child he has beautiful eyes or she has gorgeous natural curls, when we make comments solely focused on appearance-based characteristics, it can drive children to focus more on the outside than on the inside.

Children who come from hard places have often had words used against them through verbal abuse. They are not always used to hearing positive comments or receiving praise from their primary caregivers. Take the time to learn what is most important to your child and seek opportunities to authentically communicate affirmations to your child.

As a professor, I often teach practicum and internship classes where counselors in training share videos of themselves with clients. They do so with written permission from their clients in order to learn how to become more effective counselors. I often remind my students to be specific. Don't just say, "Good job!" Instead, say what is good. In the context of the counseling videos, it could be: "You did a good job demonstrating empathy to your client through your facial expressions," or "I appreciated how you used open-ended questions to elicit more information from your client."

In the context of parenting, we should also be specific with what we communicate to our children. Some examples include: "You did a good job cleaning up the first time you were asked," or "Nice work combing your hair and getting the tangles out." Also, children need to hear words of affirmation that are not associated with an action but are geared toward who they are as human beings. I think of healing words such as: "You are special," "God loves you and so do I," "You mean so much to this family."

More than anything, children seek approval from their parents, so letting your children know that you are proud of them goes a long way in encouraging them. Of course, the goal is not to teach children to please other people, but rather for them to know that they are seen, that their efforts are noticed, and that they are appreciated for who they are.

Chelsea, whose story is shared a bit later in the book, explained how Words of Affirmation is her love language. Living in a family with five siblings made it a bit difficult to know and use each love language. Sometimes loving parents who want to demonstrate love to their children don't have the time or emotional resources to do this in the way that is the most beneficial for their children. At least, they think they don't. In reality, once you learn the love languages, it's not time consuming to figure out what each of your children best responds to or even to put it into practice.

I was going over the five love languages with my then five-year-old. After briefly explaining each of them to her, I asked her which was the most meaningful to her. Without skipping a beat, she shouted out "WORDS!" It made sense. While my little girl enjoys a good snuggle, gets excited to open a present, appreciates having a task done for her, and especially enjoys our "bestie time," her face beams with pride when she hears me say things like "I'm so proud of you," "You're a good helper," and "Great job listening!" I think the reason words of affirmation mean so much to children who have been adopted is that one of the core negative distortions for these kiddos is that they were unlovable and placed for adoption because of it. Although every child greatly benefits from (needs, really) a demonstration of love in each of the five love languages, there is something significant about hearing words that tell them—and continually remind them—they are worthy.

My dear friend Dr. Anita Knight Kuhnley grew up watching *Mister Rogers' Neighborhood*, and after decades of learning lessons from Mr. Rogers, she put what she learned into a book in which she shared one of his most famous lines: "There's no person in the whole world *like you*, and I like you just the way you are."[1] Children need to know that they are special and adored. Those who have been adopted often don't feel that way, and paying particular attention to providing them with words of affirmation can go a long way in demonstrating they are dearly and deeply loved.

WORDS FROM CHILDHOOD

My father often used pet names for his five children. Some were super silly. For example, the first movie I ever saw was *Super Girl*, so Daddy started calling me Laurel from Planet Krypton. He later started to call me Scout, which was my all-time favorite nickname because Scout was the beloved, only daughter of attorney Atticus Finch in *To Kill a Mockingbird*. Since my father was also a lawyer, and we were from the Deep South, the narrative fit. I relished being called that name (though I am not implying I was my father's favorite, as he truly loved his children equally). Daddy would also call us "hon" or "sweetie." It was probably because he had four daughters and couldn't get our names straight! Even I sometimes call one of my kids by my youngest sister's name. These terms of endearment were spoken by our father in a loving manner, and they always meant a lot to me.

What about you? What words were spoken over you or about you by your parents that led you to believe you were loved? It might be that you have good examples from your own childhood that you can apply with your children. Or, in the past, you might have been wounded by words. Working through that pain, even if it requires counseling, is crucial for being able to parent effectively. As parents, we have to remember how much power our words hold. As the proverb goes, "The tongue has the power of life and death."[2]

A GOOD EXAMPLE

Yes, words have the potential to heal or to hurt. The hurt that verbal abuse or bullying can cause does not easily go away. Sometimes the wound has been so deep, a scar remains forever. Yet, when we speak words of affirmation over our children, it is like a soothing balm. The more healing words they hear, the more recovery the brain experiences. Not only does it have a positive impact on them, but the reach can have a greater result as it's modeled for them how to communicate with others in a healthier way. It's like a stone that hits the smooth surface of a calm lake causing the water to ripple.

Our children are going to take in these words we speak, and more than likely, they are going to then use those same words with others. And not just the actual words, but the tone and the delivery that accompanies those words. Jesus said, "The mouth speaks what the heart is full of."[3] If we want our children to speak good, gospel-centered words, we need to be speaking them as well. We can teach children who have been mistreated that they can heal and that the abuse of others can end with them. While the saying "hurt people hurt people" is true, we can help our children end that cycle.

KIND COMMENTS

Little Marlene craves kind comments. She longs to be told that she was chosen, that she is loved by God and her parents, and that nothing and no one will come between them. While Ruthie and Jack sometimes wonder if their words will ever be enough, they have come to understand that these words of affirmation must be repeated often lest Marlene completely forget about the truth they hold.

While some children might ignore these kinds of comments—or even roll their eyes with embarrassment—Marlene eats them up. One day, she may be able to repeat the reality of who she is, and whose she is, but for now she needs to continually be reminded of this. Marlene is not alone, as many children who have been adopted require affirming words, and not just actions, to know they are truly loved.

A FINAL THOUGHT ON WORDS

In speaking words of affirmation, remember to praise your child for effort, not for perfection. One adopted son said, "I don't ever please my father. Whatever I do is never good enough. If I make a B on my report card, he tells me I should have made an A. If I make a double in playing ball, he tells me I should have made it into a triple. Sometimes I feel like giving up." This father may have been trying to motivate his son to do his best, but what the son heard was criticism. Far better to praise a child for making a B, and a double. Then next week you can talk about what might be done to move a B to a B+ or how to stretch a double into a triple. All children need to hear words of affirmation, but if this is their primary love language, such words spell the difference between a positive relationship with their parents or a fractured relationship.

DISCOVERING A CHILD'S PRIMARY LOVE LANGUAGE

After reading about all five love languages and how they can be applied to children who have been adopted, you might be wondering how you can best identify the primary love languages of your own children.

Discovering the primary love language of an adopted child is not always easy, especially if you adopted an older child or a child from another culture. You don't have the advantage of knowing the experiences they had before they came into your family. However, though it may take longer, you can discover and learn to speak their primary love language along with the other four. Here are some practical ideas:

First, observe your child's behavior. How do they relate to you, their siblings, and other people with whom they interact? If you see them speaking affirming words, that can be a clue as to what they would like to receive. If they are giving others high fives or pats on the back, then Physical Touch may well be their love language. The love language a child speaks most often is likely their own primary love language. If you adopted a child at birth or an early age, this is the best way to discover their love language. You can discover a child's love language by the age of three or four years old by using this method.

Another approach is to give the child two options. For instance: "I have some free time this afternoon. Would you like to take a walk in the park with me, or would you like for me to write a poem about how wonderful you are and then read it to you?" One option is quality time, and the other is words of affirmation. Repeat this process using different options and keep a record of the child's responses. You will likely see one love language beginning to stand out above the others.

If your child is old enough to talk, and especially if you adopted them at an older age, you might say: "I really want to be a good mom/dad, but I need your help. Can you tell me something I could do or stop doing that would make me a better mom/dad?" Be brave and listen. If they are not yet bonding with you, they may say, "Just leave me alone," to which you might respond, "Can you give me an example of what you mean?" Their answer may give you insight into what is going on in their mind. Continue speaking all five languages as you have opportunity. Six months later, you may share the concept of the five love languages and that all of us have a primary love language. Then ask, "Which of these five is most meaningful to you?" Their answer may surprise you.

If they had foster parents in the past, you might ask, "Did your foster parents speak your love language?" Again, their answer will give you insight into their past experience. If they say, "No one has ever loved me," this gives you an opportunity to say, "Well, I want to be the first, because I really do love you, and I want to learn how best to share my love for you." If they don't give you a preference, then continue to speak all five and observe their responses. You will likely see a change in their behavior when you are speaking their primary love language.

Andrea was shown love through Gifts and Words of Affirmation when her primary love languages are Acts of Service and Quality Time. She shared, "The discrepancy between my natural love language and how my parents demonstrated love explains much of the conflict and season of feeling unloved that I experienced. I firmly believe that my adoptive parents did love me, despite the pain I felt as a child, which highlights the importance of exploring your child's natural love lens. Had my parents received this guidance, the love in our home could have been more clearly manifested!"

We believe that understanding the love language concept and seeking ways to speak all five languages while focusing on the child's primary language will help you be more effective in meeting the child's emotional need for love.

10

Challenging Circumstances

NOW THAT WE HAVE gone through the five love languages, we want to turn our attention to some challenging or unique adoption situations. This chapter will cover adopting solo and single parenting, marriage/divorce/remarriage, stepparenting, and even when parents are not on the same parenting page. All these special circumstances will impact the adoptive parenting journey, and we hope this will be helpful to those of you in these particular positions.

MY TIME AS A SOLO PARENT

I've never been a single mom, but I have solo parented. As others who have spouses in the military or who travel extensively for work know, when your parenting partner is away from home, everything falls to you. During the approximately six months my husband was deployed in 2020, with COVID spreading like wildfire and my father seriously ill, all the caregiving duties for our infant son and toddler daughter were my responsibility. This was a stressful time—not only did I have to meet their physical and emotional needs (which are many at their ages), I never experienced a real break from parenting obligations. If something came up at the children's school, I was the only parent who could be contacted. Their preschool wasn't always open, so I would spend two weeks at a time caring for both children while working full-time without childcare. I managed all their healthcare decisions and decisions about discipline for our older child. Once, all three of us had a twenty-four-hour stomach virus. Thankfully, the symptoms didn't hit all of us at once, so I was able to care for one child before I got sick and the other child after I got through the worst of my own illness.

These are daily scenarios for many parents who have been solo parenting (by choice or not) far longer than I did and in much harder circumstances. Some parents go years without a break. This is often the case when a single person adopts or a couple adopts, but later divorces. There are several ways a parent may come to raising adopted kids solo, and we'll look at these more in depth in the next section. As difficult as it may be, it's possible for a single parent to successfully adopt and raise a child.

ADOPTING SOLO AND SINGLE PARENTING

Many parents would agree that the best situation for a child is to be born to and raised by a loving, married husband and wife. Most would also agree that when this is not the case, being raised by a loving single person is far better than being raised in a dysfunctional home. I have a dear friend who is raising two children she adopted after they were removed from their biological parents, a married couple who neglected and abused them.

Her single status does not change the fact that she is a capable and competent parent. As recently as 2019, the data shows that nearly 25 percent of adoptive families consist of a single mother, and 3 percent of adoptive families include a single father.[1] While the majority of children who have been adopted are raised by married couples, over a quarter of adoptive families should not be overlooked simply because there are not two parents in the home. Certainly, being with one loving parent is a much better scenario for the child than being in an unhealthy home.

Since many adoption agencies (in particular Christian agencies) require adoptive parents to be married couples, the majority of single parents, primarily women, choose to foster and adopt children from state foster care systems. A strong social network, financial stability, and job flexibility are several needs solo adoptive parents should ideally have in place prior to adopting.[2] When all the parenting falls on one person, raising children can be twice as exhausting! So, how can single parents raise adopted children well? Before I answer that, I'd like you to hear about some women who have taken this challenge on and given a child a new life.

HELPFUL STORIES

Sarah dreamt her whole life of becoming a mother and had plans to be married with at least one child by age thirty. When that didn't happen, she became angry with God. Yet, He stirred her heart toward foster care, and she soon had a fifteen-month-old little girl placed with her, with whom she immediately bonded. Despite this, she struggled with deciding whether to move forward with adoption because she was single and had no local family to support her.

After months of crying herself to sleep, some wise advice from a trusted friend reminded her of the truth she already knew: she and the little girl were already a family. Despite the potential health problems this child had, Sarah moved forward with adopting her daughter, Erin. While it was not easy to be a single parent, Sarah said it is 100 percent possible for those called to this. She also said, "If I had a biological child, I would never turn myself away from her should she be given a diagnosis. Erin was my daughter and so was everything that makes her who she is."

Adoptive mother Rebecca always wanted to adopt. By the age of twelve, she envisioned becoming a pilot and flying around the world adopting kids in need. She eventually realized that was not very realistic, and later, she pursued working in the adoption field, which took her to Romania. That is where, at the age of twenty-seven, Rebecca (still single) adopted her first child, a seven-year-old girl. Rebecca and her daughter lived in Romania for another two years, where she navigated life as a solo parent.

MARRIAGE, DIVORCE, REMARRIAGE, AND STEPPARENTING AFTER ADOPTION

Marriage, divorce, remarriage, and stepparenting all exist within the adoption community as much as they do outside of it. Remember Sarah from the last section? The Lord did answer her desire to be married, which resulted in her daughter soon having a stepfather. He would go on to adopt Erin and become her father, yet there were some adjustments that had to be made after the move from a one-parent to a two-parent home. Now, Erin's parents are working together to determine how best to approach raising their daughter. Rebecca also married. She and her husband had two biological children and also adopted five children together. That makes for a total of eight children!

Sometimes, the best-laid plans and intentions go awry. Jennifer was thrilled when she and her husband adopted a baby soon after marriage. They knew they could not have biological children and didn't wait long to begin the process of adoption. Unfortunately, when their child was a few years old, Jennifer's husband pursued a relationship outside of their marriage. Jennifer was devastated that her marriage was ending but felt even worse about the impact this would have on their child, who had already lost two parents and was now losing two more parents, at least part of the time.

Through mediation and counseling, Jennifer and her soon-to-be ex-husband were able to come up with a visitation plan, and Jennifer was committed to doing everything she could to ensure her young child experienced love. Years down the road, Jennifer remarried. Her ex-husband was already remarried by this time. This meant the child now had two biological parents, two adoptive parents, and two stepparents. That is a lot of parents to navigate, and children need support in doing so, which might include family counseling. An invaluable resource for this type of circumstance is the book *Building Love Together in Blended Families: The 5 Love Languages and Becoming Stepfamily Smart.*[3]

WHEN PARENTS ARE NOT ON THE SAME PAGE

Parenting is never easy, even for the most like-minded couples. Throw in the challenges of adoption, and parenting can get even harder. For some moms and dads, this looks like not agreeing on how best to even approach parenting. My husband, Nick, was raised, in part, by a Marine ("Once a Marine, always a Marine!"). Nick was always a good kid, but on the occasion that he wasn't "in line," his father's military approach to parenting shaped him up quickly. As a young man, Nick joined the Navy. Like father, like son. Now that he has a son, Nick is finding that taking a hard line is not always the best approach.

Parenting a child with big emotions, which may be rooted in what happened to our baby boy in utero, takes a great deal of patience and empathy. You can't simply tell every child to behave or suffer the consequences, and then expect the behavior to immediately improve. While that often worked with Nick as a child (same for me), that approach doesn't work with our son. Yes, our child needs parents who are firm and loving, like Nick's dad was. But our son also needs gentle and positive parenting, rooted in trust and safety.

When a child is raised by a loving biological parent, attachment happens more naturally. With an adopted child, developing secure attachment must be more intentional. Nick has a desire to master how to modify what he learned growing up for the benefit of his child, and I am certainly not afraid to share with him what I learn. Thankfully, we are both willing to receive the information and change as a result. Even so, we are not always on the same parenting page.

The same is true for Kristen and John. Because they, like all parents, don't always agree, they have some ground rules in place to help them navigate bumps in the parenting road. One of those ground rules is that they do not correct one another in front of other people or their children. Once they are alone, either Kristen or John will initiate the conversation by stating, "Help me understand your position." Making assumptions about how things should go within parenting is often a trigger for disagreements. Instead of making these assumptions, parents should communicate more openly up front.

Jeanie and Nate agree that communication can help avoid conflict. Jeanie gave the example of her husband's desire to watch their kids play outside while she desires him to be more intentional and structured in his interactions. She becomes frustrated because she wants him to do something different and he becomes frustrated because he feels she is being judgmental. Jeanie says that when she can make a few specific requests of her husband, he often receives and implements those suggestions. For example, Nate responds to requests such as going to the park, playing baseball in the yard, running an errand together, going to their girls' rooms to hug and kiss them good night, etc. Jeanie also notes that giving and responding to parenting suggestions goes both ways.

CULTURAL DIFFERENCES

When we explore the love languages, culture needs to be considered. In a biological family, the culture is shared, but when a family story includes adoption, cultures often come together. I have friends who have adopted from various countries, including China, Ghana, Haiti, and Russia. Other friends, who are Caucasian American, have adopted African American children—and vice versa. According to the U.S. Department of Health and Human Services, "fewer than one-third (28 percent) of all adoptions in 2017–2019 were transracial. Of these transracial adoptions, 90 percent involved children of color adopted by parents of a different race."[4]

You need look no further than social media to learn about diverse families developed through adoption. I shared about Sarah earlier in this chapter. We discussed her experiences as a white woman adopting a black child. One aspect of culture she needed to learn was how to care for her daughter's hair. She specifically sought out advice from African American friends. Learning about the culture of your child's biological family can demonstrate your love and care for every aspect of your child. Helping an adopted child learn about their cultural and racial history, struggles, traditions, food, holidays, clothing, and more can help them remain connected to their heritage while also clearly indicating to the child that the goal is not to rob them of their culture, but to respect the culture in which they were born and learn about it together.

Parts of Sophie's story have been shared throughout this book. She and her sister are from the same country, and Sophie says she appreciates having someone in her life who is coming from a similar circumstance. Children who have been adopted benefit from connecting with others from their own cultural background. This often takes intentionality on the part of parents. Rebecca and her husband, who adopted six children from all over the world, have tried to create an environment that is supportive of their kids. This includes taking trips to home countries; providing ethnic mentors; filling their home with food, art, and books that reflect the cultures of their children; and being responsive to the discrimination their children have experienced. Rebecca shared that when she and her husband mess up and aren't culturally responsive, they own it and apologize. They also recognize the importance of being intentional about creating a diverse community.

Andrea, an adult adoptee, also encourages parents to honor, explore, and value their child's cultural heritage. This includes immersing children in communities where their heritage is represented, connecting the children with elders from that cultural background, challenging your own cultural assumptions, and seeking out and listening to voices of adult adoptees from your child's cultural heritage.

RUTHIE AND JACK: GETTING ON THE SAME PAGE

Ruthie and Jack are not always on the same parenting page. What couple is? Yet, they are committed to working together to raise their children the best they can. They recognize that their children have needs that other children may not have. For instance, they understand that counseling needs to be a regular part of their lives.

When one parent does not like how the other one is parenting, they take the time to address the concern in private so as not to undermine the other parent. Sometimes when Marlene and Jack are squabbling, Ruthie will intervene with a gentle "Hey, what's going on here?" Ruthie is often able to help get daddy and daughter back on track without making it appear that she is parenting Jack. Jack appreciates the help! Likewise, when Marlene is being clingy with Ruthie during times when Ruthie is really not available, Jack helps to distract Marlene, and they both enjoy their time together.

Parenting is a partnership, regardless of how you come to parent your children. However, parents need to understand the unique challenges (and blessings) that come along with parenting children through adoption. Ruthie and Jack continue to take steps necessary to develop their knowledge and learn how best to apply what they have learned as they raise Marlene and her sister.

All About Siblings

ONE MORNING BEFORE the kids headed out for school, I sat
with one child on each side of me. They each tried to push the
other one off, saying that I was "theirs." As they were escalating
and shouting "my mommy" to one another, my husband inter-
vened and helped me separate them as I attempted to assure each
of them that I loved them both deeply and equally. To be sure,
sibling rivalry and conflict in general goes on in lots of families,
but sometimes this looks a bit different—and a bit more complicated—in adoptive families.

Jeanie shared that when she compliments one of her daughters, the other one will seek a compliment as well. Instead of affirming them in the exact same ways, Jeanie seeks to help her children understand there are things special and unique about each
of them and that she loves and appreciates them equally despite
their differences.

Chelsea was born in and adopted from Romania, alongside
a boy. This pair of kiddos were not biologically related and were
born eleven days apart, yet, Chelsea explained, they were raised as
twins. Their parents wound up adopting four children from Russia; one was six when she was adopted and did not speak English.
For this family, "adoption was very normal." Because Chelsea was

the oldest, she took on a second-mom role, and she acknowledges there was some sibling conflict in her home as well.

Jealousy between siblings is not uncommon, but addressing the envy that children who have been adopted experience is not always as simple as teaching them to be grateful for what they have. No, they need to know that they are truly one of a kind and don't have to be like others or want to be like others. Many children who come to be adopted were in foster homes prior to coming into their adoptive family's home. The shuffling around can contribute to feelings of rejection, even in the best of foster care circumstances. Wondering why others get "picked" when you don't is a common reaction among these children, and it can stir up feelings of insecurity and jealousy. This doesn't just go away when a child enters their permanent home, and children must learn how to interact in a forever family as they become more secure in their place.

HANNAH'S STORY

While attending an out-of-state adoption conference, I enjoyed meeting and spending time with other adoptive parents. I was able to have some conversations with one particular couple during break times and learned about their journey to adoption. They had several biological children and one child by adoption from birth. Despite their daughter Hannah being with them from the start of her life, she never quite felt like she belonged. Her parents shared that she took most of their time and attention and that they found their other children "easy" compared to her. They could not figure out a way to break through to her and help resolve the rivalry she felt with her siblings. No amount of telling her she was chosen and loved could convince her of this truth.

They came to the conference wondering what they could—and should—do to best help their precious elementary-age child. (Perhaps you are wondering the same about your child.) Throughout the conference, they were reminded not only to tell their adopted daughter she was loved just as much as their biological children, but to continue to *show* her that she was loved just as much. Making empathetic statements about their daughter's circumstances (e.g., "We hear you when you say that you feel loved less than the other children because you're the only one who was adopted"), while also communicating the messages through that child's love language, would go a long way in helping to demonstrate the truth of the words they had been speaking for years.

SISTERS, SISTERS

One of my favorite movies is *White Christmas*. One scene in this 1954 classic shows two sisters performing a song called "Sisters." The lyrics reveal that the sisters are devoted to each other—as long as a man doesn't come between them. It's a fun song and dance routine made even more comical when a short while later, two military veterans wind up doing the same routine in an attempt to help the sisters get out of town quick. The whole movie is delightful, but this song reminds me of the unique bond between sisters. This is certainly the case for Sophie and her sister.

Both adopted from Russia, but years apart and from different cities, they discovered their birth mothers had the same first name. Sophie said having a sister is "great" and "a blessing." She longed to have a sister because she had seen others with siblings, and thought, "I want one of those!" Her sister struggles with special needs, and it can be challenging for the family, but it's also a learning experience for Sophie. For her, it had been a blessing to have someone at home who is younger, someone she can guide. Sophie shared: "We get along so well, and it's eye-opening to have someone be there who you know you can count on." Sophie also says that the way their parents teach and lead her young sister is a huge inspiration for how she wants to parent her own children one day. "They are so patient with her. It's how I want to be," she said.

THE IMPACT OF BIRTH ORDER

I was the third-born child of my parents, who had already had a son (their firstborn) and a daughter. After me came two more girls. So, my mama and daddy raised a son and four daughters— and I was smack dab in the middle. There is often this notion that if you have one son and one daughter, your family "should" be complete, but my parents wanted a big family. And a big family we had! Of course, there are pros and cons to that, but I am grateful for what I experienced and learned as a result of being raised along with four siblings.

According to many researchers, birth order matters. Dr. Alfred Adler is credited as being the person who developed the birth order theory during his career as a medical doctor and psychotherapist in the early 1900s. He believed that "the order in which a child is born shapes their development and personality."[1] For example, oldest children have a lot of expectations placed on them, their parents are often stricter with them than with younger children, and they are expected to show more responsibility. As a result, according to Adler's research, firstborn children often have solid leadership skills. The middle child is said to be the peacekeeper and the one who likes negotiation and compromise. Or perhaps the middle child is the one who, seeking to carve out a place for him or herself, is more rebellious or attention seeking. The youngest child is the baby. Adler believed youngest children would take one of two paths: the successful, go-to person in the family or the avoidant, low-confidence one. At the same time, this child knows his or her place in the family—as the baby!

We can't forget about the "only child." While I was the middle of five children, my husband was raised an only child. Adler believed that only children are often intelligent and creative, but sometimes stubborn or reluctant to share.[2] My husband is smart as a whip, and he is also set in his ways!

Birth order matters within the adoptive world too. While it's not always possible, and sometimes families are called to do otherwise, many adoptive families seek to maintain birth order within their home. This means that when you have a child who is, for example, six years old, you would not bring in a child older than six. Or if you have a thirteen-year-old, you will only bring in children younger than thirteen. It can get a bit challenging when a child comes into your home as the baby in your family when he or she is the oldest in their birth family or vice versa.

It's important for parents to be mindful of the impact former and current birth order may have on a child's attitude and behavior. For example, if a child is used to being the oldest and "in charge" and is then adopted into a home where they are no longer in that position, it might be a difficult transition for the child to make. Maintaining a child's birth order might be helpful for them as they live outside of their biological family's home, but even when that is not possible, simply being aware of birth order can aid the parent and child in understanding more about why they act as they do. Of course, so much of the birth order theory is rooted in how a child is reared. How they are nurtured in the home as a sibling is going to outweigh the impact of whether they are an oldest, middle, or youngest child.

ADOPTING BIOLOGICAL SIBLINGS

Like Jeanie and Nate, Cindy adopted biological siblings, except she did it solo. There is something sacred about keeping biological siblings together when possible. In both these families' cases, their children had at least one connection to their biological family. There was at least one person in their life who shared their DNA, who looked like them, and who shared memories (including the hard ones). This doesn't mean that the children act or think alike. My own siblings are biological, and though we love each other deeply and share DNA, we don't act or think alike!

But in the case of Cindy, one of the struggles was the depth of memories that the elder child had compared to the younger one. Another struggle was the connection the older one felt to their former life and even to the biological parents, who were abusive and neglectful. A third challenge is that while both children have special needs, the younger one has a greater level of need and is not able to understand or process much of the past experiences. So, Cindy constantly has to navigate helping her children cope with what they have been through, at different developmental levels.

When adopting a sibling group, parents must understand that just because children come from the same biological parents (whether one or both parents), they will still each be unique, and how parents interact with each child will vary depending on a number of factors.

The Sibling Interaction and Behavior Study (also known as SIBS), conducted by the University of Minnesota, followed children in six hundred families starting in 1999 and determined that "their relationships with their brothers and sisters (whether adopted or the biological children of the adoptive parents) were as close and loving as those between bio-siblings."[3]

USING THE LOVE LANGUAGES WITH SIBLINGS

It's worth reiterating that each child needs to receive all five of the love languages. Regardless of whether a primary and secondary love language have yet been identified (which typically happens by the age of four), all children need to be shown love through Acts of Service, Gifts, Physical Touch, Quality Time, and Words of Affirmation.

As previously noted, when there is more than one child in a family, it can seem a bit daunting to individually use all of these with each child, and even more so to focus on using what a particular child best responds to. Yet it is possible. Examples have been given throughout the book, but here are a few more:

Acts of Service
- Work together as a team with your children to clean up the playroom.
- Surprise each child once a week by completing one of their chores.
- Create a photo book or box for each of them containing photos of the two of you so that they can be reminded of how special they are to you.

- Do something that would demonstrate to your child that you loved them enough to do this just for them, as an act of service.

Gifts

- When going shopping, pick out one small item for each child, even if it is a pack of chewing gum or a one-dollar toy.
- Select something that you know each child likes. If selecting different items will cause jealousy, stick to the exact same item for each child; but (if possible) write their name on their items so each child knows which is theirs. (My mother used to have to do this with our clothes hangers!)
- If you go on a trip, bring back a souvenir for each of your children. I have brought back small items from conferences, and my kids loved them as much as they would a big gift.

Physical Touch

- Have your children swap off riding on your back across the room and back.
- Take turns hugging your children, counting out loud to ten for each child so that they know you are hugging them an equal amount of time.
- Take a walk while holding the hand of each of your children.
- Wrap your child up in a blanket and snuggle with him or her.
- Twirl your daughter like a ballerina.
- Hoist your son above your head.

Quality Time

- Commit to spending at least ten minutes a day with each child during which you get into a child ego state (basically, a child-like state) and play whatever the child requests (within reason, of course). This is the essence of Mind, Body, and Soul Time, introduced in chapter 8.
- If you have another child or children, first get them focused on something else. In a two-parent home with two children, this might look like Mom spending time with child A while Dad spends time with child B, and then you switch.
- In a single parent home with three children, two children could be asked to read or allotted twenty minutes of screen time while you spend quality time with the other child, cultivating their hobby or interest. Rotate so that each child gets ten minutes with you and twenty minutes of reading/screen time.

Words of Affirmation

- Compliment each child in front of their siblings. Make sure to do this equally so that each child knows they are loved and that you love their siblings, without triggering any fear that one child is loved more than the other.
- Praise your child for working hard, using self-control, or helping around the house.
- Tell them you love them simply for who they are!

MARLENE AND HER BABY SISTER

Some of Marlene's struggles appear to be rooted in sibling rivalry. Even though she seems to like her baby sister, the issue is really about her questioning her place in the family. *Do her parents still love her? Do they love her as much as they used to? Do they love the new baby more than they love her? If they loved her so much, why did they have a new baby?* By using the five love languages, her parents not only reassure her that they love her, but they assure her that they love her as much as they always have (if not more) and that they always will. They will also bolster her in her role as big sister.

It's likely that Marlene will continue to have moments of insecurity in her home because of there being another child taking up some of her parents' time and attention. Ruthie and Jack will have to continue maintaining a strong bond with their daughters and helping their girls connect with one another.

12

Adoption Support

OVER THE YEARS, I HAVE seen people rally around those who are adopting in beautiful ways. I think of the family that came alongside a single mom who was adopting a traumatized child. They have included this mom and her daughter in everything from holiday gatherings to globe-trotting vacations. Another couple found themselves suddenly with a newborn. The mom explained that members of her church's small group have loaded her up with necessities, helped care for the baby during the day so Mom could sleep, and even provided a nightly dinner, complete with kitchen cleanup! A local church in my area has what they call an adoption and foster care closet, and they invite families in either of those processes to come and help themselves to whatever they need. These are but a few examples of how people and communities can help adoptive families.

Sometimes, though, the support is simply not there. One single adoptive mom shared how even her own family would make comments like "You chose this" when she asked them for help. From my own experience, folks did the best they could to help me during the extremely challenging time of caring for a newly adopted son and my older daughter during a pandemic and while my husband was deployed. I think about those who have no help, and my heart aches for them.

While it's certainly true that all new parents need help and support, there are some unique challenges that adoptive families face. Sometimes a family receives a child into their home without any notice. I have known several couples that received a call to come get a baby from the hospital immediately! One was told by the case worker, "I don't have any information except it's a newborn girl. Do you want to come get her?" My friend immediately, and in faith, said yes. She then had to stop on the way to the hospital to purchase a car seat! When a woman is pregnant, she has time to prepare, but that is not always the case for those adopting. These families may be in last-minute need of food, furniture, diapers, clothes, bottles, a car seat, and other items. There is also the need for help with regular everyday duties so that more time can be spent bonding with the new child. And, sometimes, there is a need for respite care so that the parent can have a break and catch a breath, due to the fatigue and anxiety that come with parenting, especially in these special circumstances.

Moms and dads, don't be afraid to ask for help. You might get turned down by someone (or more than one), but don't let that deter you from asking someone else. Explore which churches in your community explicitly support adoptive families. Ask the local adoption agencies or state social service department for assistance. Seek out support groups, whether online or in person. Attend online classes or in-person conferences. There are many opportunities for receiving the training and support you need. You have to start somewhere.

Kristen and John started a blog about their adoption journey and tried to keep friends and family informed every step of the way. Most specifically, they requested intentional prayer. They experienced power through those prayers and found that God met every one of their needs during the wait. While finances were certainly one need, they found that this was not their greatest need. Instead, what they needed far more was strength and endurance that could only come from their faith in God. While that strength can only come through faith, parents still need others to support them on this journey.

HOW TO CONNECT WITH ADOPTIVE PARENTS

Adoption is not neat and tidy. There are raw and painful moments and experiences, regardless of how the adoption came to be. Adoptive families need people who are going to be supportive and who are going to cheer them on. Negative comments, like those below, are not at all helpful:

"Aren't you afraid her 'real' mother will come back for her one day?"

"I heard about this adopted kid who assaulted his sister, and the adoptive parents gave him back."

"Those kids are broken. Are you sure you can handle their trauma?"

I remember being asked about the mother of one of my children. My response was, "I am the mother." Then the reply came, "You know what I mean—the real mother." I chose then to kindly clarify: "Actually, I don't know what you mean because I am the real mother. Are you referring to the biological mother?" No, those certainly aren't the comments to make and questions to ask. Neither are invasive questions about a child's backstory. It's not anyone's business unless they are someone who needs to know for the benefit of the child. It's also not acceptable to constantly note that a child is adopted. I have heard, "This is Laurel and her adopted children" on a number of occasions. This isn't acceptable when referring to single adoptive parents either. Some people do this to make it clear to others that these solo parents didn't have children outside of marriage. In most cases, the only person who cares what others think is the one sharing the private adoption information.

Adoption is nothing to be ashamed of. Sometimes people share an adoption status because they're proud of you for following the God-given call to adopt. Adoption should not be a secret. Yet, those who are not a part of someone's adoption story should remember that it is not their story to tell. Allow the adoptive family to share that information how they choose and with whomever they choose.

Chelsea shared that her mother used humor to address and defuse rude questions. (This reminds me of my friend who has a big family. When someone would say to her "better you than me," she would reply with a huge grin, "I agree!") Chelsea and her siblings always knew they were adopted and appreciated the transparency. Because of this, they were comfortable asking their parents questions, and their parents never shut down those inquiries. Chelsea says it's important for people to support children who have been adopted by taking time to really get to know them and to ask them age-appropriate questions in order to learn how they most feel cared for.

Rebecca says that a primary reason that adoptive families need to connect with other adoptive families is because they need empathy. They need other parents who are farther along in the adoption journey to advise them. Children, too, need to know other adoptive children so that they don't feel so alone.

HOW TO CONNECT WITH ADOPTED CHILDREN

Children who have been adopted, regardless of the age at which they were adopted, often need counseling services to help them with the various thoughts, feelings, and behaviors that accompany their experiences. Trust-Based Relational Interventions has already been mentioned throughout this book as a recommended treatment of choice. Play therapy is another powerful treatment modality. Play therapy is not the same as spontaneous play; rather, it is systematic and therapeutic.[1] Trained play therapists "help clients prevent or resolve psychosocial difficulties and achieve optimal growth and development."[2] While many mental health professionals use play, registered play therapists (RPTs) meet the highest level of training and credentials in the therapeutic use of play.

A third form of treatment that can be helpful for parents and children is parent-child interaction therapy (PCIT),[3] "an evidence-based behavior parent training treatment for young children with emotional and behavioral disorders that places emphasis on improving the quality of the parent-child relationship and changing parent-child interaction patterns."[4] Keep in mind that sometimes when a child presents with symptoms and behaviors indicative of disorders such as attention deficit hyperactivity disorder (ADHD) or oppositional defiant disorder, he or she is acting out from a place of trauma, not from an actual neurological disorder. Nevertheless, the intended outcomes from any of these three treatment options—TBRI, RPT, and PCIT—include increased attachment and connection as well as a decrease in negative symptoms and behaviors.

One of the best pieces of advice on how other people can love adopted children well comes from Jeannie, a foster care worker and adoptive mother of three. She reminds people to be understanding of behavioral issues and not to compare children who have been adopted to other children of the same age. Not everyone comes from the same background, and no child should ever be made to feel like they must live up to the unrealistic expectations of others.

Andrea, an adult adoptee, shared that honoring the child's story and the fact that it is rooted in the trauma of separation is critical to supporting them. Additional advice is to learn about and support their unique developmental challenges, hold space for their grief without allowing it to feel personal to the adoptive parent, encourage the child to be who God created them to be, and rejoice in their being wonderfully made by God.

PRIZING YOUR CHILDREN

Dr. Carl Rogers (1902–1987) was an American psychologist who developed what is now called Person Centered Therapy (PCT). One of the core conditions of PCT is unconditional positive regard. Rogers wrote that this "means there are no conditions of acceptance" and involves caring for someone as a separate person, rather than in a possessive way.[5] Psychologist John Dewey coined the term "prizing," which Rogers used to help further describe unconditional positive regard.[6] Although this work focused on clients in counseling or psychotherapy, we should also prize our children.

As noted earlier, even children who come to us as infants have experienced wounds that could contribute to some difficult feelings and behaviors. While not all actions should be accepted, the child—as an image bearer of Christ—should be. This does not mean ignoring harmful behaviors, but it does mean demonstrating love to children, even when they are wayward. Again, many of the behaviors these children exhibit are directly related to the trauma they have experienced. Connecting with your children in a loving, safe, and trusting manner while also seeking out professional assistance can have lifelong benefits. What better way to show your children you prize them than by doing everything within your power and control to help your family?

RESOURCES FOR ADOPTIVE FAMILIES

Fortunately, there are many resources (and growing) available for adoptive families. There is no one place where you can have all your needs met, but there are many available. At the end of this book, you'll find a list that contains blogs, books, conferences, ministries, podcasts, and websites that can assist adoptive families as they navigate this unique journey. This list is certainly not exhaustive, but it will provide you with a starting point.

In addition, many churches have adoption and foster care ministries, including support groups and "closets" that contain all the necessities a family would need to be able to take in a child needing placement. A simple online search should reveal which churches close to you have an adoption ministry.

It's also imperative that you seek early intervention for children who come from hard places. Don't wait until problems feel insurmountable. Start early with assessments and treatment for occupational therapy, physical therapy, mental health counseling with a trauma-informed licensed professional (preferably one who has been through Trust-Based Relational Intervention training), and speech therapy. For example, as a result of his start in life, my son experienced difficulty eating solid foods. He had feeding therapy with an amazing speech therapist, and it wasn't long before he was eating us out of house and home. Educational needs also need to be considered, and I recommend that you explore all possible educational opportunities and do what you can to select what will work best for each of your children (and not just what others think you should do).

Parents who have adopted should connect with others who have "been there, done that." While each situation is unique, there are still some universal qualities to the adoption process. I recall one particularly difficult night with one of my children while my husband was deployed. After a rough time, I called my friend Cynthia, a fellow PhD counselor/professor and mother via adoption. I needed to lament and also receive her calming words of wisdom. I have turned to her many times, as she has been on this journey longer and her children are older than mine. I have also received significant support from other friends. Though they may not have children of their own or their children are biological, they have been willing to listen to me, pray with me, and even babysit on occasion. We all need support networks like this. I also strive to support them in whatever way I can.

Friends are an important resource!

SUPPORTING YOURSELF—SELF-CARE AND BRAIN SPACE

As a licensed professional counselor, licensed marriage and family therapist, and licensed social worker, I am well versed in the concept of self-care. Every conference I have ever attended addressed this in some form, and I have always talked about self-care with my students and clients. At times, I bet I start to sound like Charlie Brown's teacher. You know the droning sound she makes? Wah, wah, wah wah. I see the bleary looks on their faces. In fact, when I hear the term *self-care*, I sometimes roll my eyes as well. Who has the time for self-care? Here's the reality: we have to make time. We must take care of ourselves in order to take care of anyone else.

Self-care isn't necessarily about going to a spa or even taking a vacation; it's about taking care of ourselves emotionally, physically, and spiritually. You might keep a running list in the notes app on your phone, and use it to keep track of everything you are currently involved in. When you start to feel overwhelmed and like you have too much going on, go back to that list to see what can come off your plate. This may help you emotionally feel like you can breathe a little easier.

Physically, I know how necessary adequate sleep is to our health. I don't always make time to get enough sleep, but I do have a goal of trying to start my shut-eye at 11 p.m. Another way I care for myself physically is through fitness and the guidance of a personal trainer who is highly qualified. Exercise helps not only with weight management but also with flexibility, muscle strength, and stress reduction. My trainer reminds me that one day my grandchildren will want me to play on the floor with them, and I have to work on my physical health now in order to be available to them later on.

Spiritually, I take time to read and study my Bible, attend Sunday school and corporate worship services, and pray, often using a prayer journal. Another significant way I take care of myself is by spending time with friends. Whether it's having a cup of coffee together, seeing a play, or going on a girls' trip (usually combined with a conference), these activities lift my mood and get my mind off the stress in my life.

As parents, when we take care of our own needs, we are modeling the importance of this for our children. Besides, we cannot give out of an empty cup. Think about how you feel when you don't get enough sleep: Are you more or less likely to be patient with your children? What about when you haven't been eating healthy food frequently enough or when your stress levels are too high? Sometimes there are things that don't take up a tremendous amount of our time, but they take up a lot of brain space. We must be able to let go of things, even if it's just for the parenting season because our children need us.

Children who have been adopted have even more needs—some that only become evident the longer they are with us. We have to leave margin or bandwidth in our busy lives for counseling, speech therapy, tutoring, or anything else that arises. So, parents, take care of yourselves so that you are able to take care of your kiddos!

13

Faith Matters

AS I MENTIONED EARLIER, when our son was six weeks old, the world shut down due to the COVID pandemic. Because of this, we didn't get to celebrate his adoption in the same way we had celebrated our daughter's. On our son's adoption day, we loaded up the baby and went to the attorney's office, where we sat in a room meeting the judge via an online meeting platform. We ordered takeout from a nice restaurant on the way home and celebrated as a family of four. It was a sweet time, but a far cry from a few years earlier and the large gatherings we had to celebrate our first adoption.

That evening after the kids were in bed, I shared the news of his finalized adoption on my social media accounts. And for the first time, with almost 25,000 likes, I had a tweet go somewhat viral. That resulted in our being contacted for a magazine interview, and we were able to share our story about what it was like to adopt during the pandemic. The Lord redeemed my disappointment about us not being able to celebrate our little boy in the traditional way by blowing the traditional celebration out of the water. It felt so affirming to have so many congratulate us and rejoice with us over what the Lord had done. Truly, this story is not about us, but about what God is doing. Adoption is a place where

135

joy and sorrow meet. It is also biblical, and we want to share a few biblical adoption stories as we wrap up with this final chapter.

ADOPTION STORIES IN THE BIBLE

We started this book sharing about how adoption is near to the heart of God. In fact, the Bible has numerous examples of adoption. We'll cover three here in this final chapter. The first is the adoption of Moses by Pharaoh's daughter, the second is the adoption of Esther by her cousin Mordecai, and the third is the adoption of Jesus by Joseph. Moses and Esther are biblical heavyweights in their own right, but knowing Jesus was adopted should assure all of us that even when we can't understand it, adoption is a part of God's plan. First, let's look at Moses.

You likely know the basics of this story found in the book of Exodus, chapter 2. After Jochebed gave birth to a baby boy, she hid him for three months so that he would not be killed during a time when Pharaoh had ordered all newborn Hebrew boys to be murdered. When Jochebed could no longer hide the baby, she placed a basket (that she waterproofed!) among the reeds along the bank of the Nile. She laid the baby in the basket, and his sister watched to see what would happen. When Pharaoh's daughter—an Egyptian—went down to the Nile to bathe, she saw the basket and had one of her servants retrieve it. The New International Version says that when she opened the basket and saw a crying baby, "she felt sorry for him" (verse 6) despite knowing he was a Hebrew baby. The baby's sister (assumed to be Miriam) asked Pharaoh's daughter if she should go and get a Hebrew woman to nurse the baby. When given the go-ahead, Miriam retrieved Jochebed, who was paid by Pharaoh's daughter to nurse the baby until he got older, at which point Jochebed "took him to Pharaoh's daughter and he became her son" (verse 10). The Bible says that it was Pharaoh's daughter who named him Moses because that word sounds like "drew out," and she had drawn him out of the water.[1]

In this adoption story, the biological mother knew the adoptive mother, but the adoptive mother did not know who the birth mother was. It's not clear exactly when Moses went to live with Pharaoh's daughter. Could he have gotten to know his sister Miriam and brother Aaron during the time he was being nursed by Jochebed? Yes, but the Bible is not clear about how he came to know them as siblings. Certainly, there was no DNA matching or ancestry websites to help Moses out. There had to have been some degree of openness within these families for it all to come together as it did. There is an obvious love that Jochebed had for the little boy she gave birth to in order to protect him the way she did. She actually took him to Pharaoh's daughter when it was time. There's little doubt that this was heart-wrenching, and at the same time she would have known this was the only way to save her son's life.

That sounds a lot like the stories of many birth mothers who choose the same path forward for their children, placing their children with moms and dads who are more capable of giving them what they need. This is, of course, not always the way adoption comes about. Another interesting aspect to the story of Moses is the fact that he was born Hebrew but raised Egyptian. Being born in one culture, or even subculture, and raised in another is not uncommon these days, but it was during the time of Moses' upbringing.

My daughter loves hearing the story of Moses, and she asks for it to be read to her over and over. Knowing that she is not alone and that God can and does use children who have been adopted to do great big things has been inspirational to her. Of course, Moses is not the only adopted hero in the Bible. Let's look now to the second example: Mordecai and Esther.

The Bible doesn't provide much background on this older/younger cousin set turned father/daughter. What we do know is that Mordecai took Esther as his own daughter after her parents died. We also know that they were very close. The first piece of evidence is the trust that Esther had in Mordecai. For example, Esther never revealed her people or family because Mordecai had directed her not to do so. The second piece of evidence for their closeness is that after Esther was taken to the king's harem, Mordecai walked daily near the courtyard to find out what was happening to her. Third, even after Esther was declared queen, she "was still following Mordecai's directions, just as she did when she lived in his home."[2] There is an apparent mutual care and concern between them. Esther very much respects her older cousin and adoptive father and trusts Mordecai enough to follow his advice to go before the king, even at the risk of her own death. In fact, it is Mordecai who states the well-known words, "Who knows if perhaps you were made queen for such a time as this?"[3]

Moses was adopted by a nonrelative while Esther was adopted by a relative (which, today, is called kinship care or kinship placement prior to adoption). Both circumstances are more common today. The third adoption story—the adoption of Jesus—will never be replicated. On the surface, He had a birth mother and a stepfather (His only earthly father), who raised Him as his own. But there is more to the story in the Christian faith. Jesus is the Son of God. He *is* God, as one of the three members of the Holy Trinity. While Mary was His mother, carried Him in her womb, and delivered Him in Bethlehem, God is His Father. God made

Joseph the earthly father of Jesus. We think of Joseph as a stepfather in modern terms, but surely, he was solely looked at as *father* during the days of Mary and Joseph raising Jesus.

While these ancient adoptions did not involve lawyers and loads of paperwork, they are still clear examples of a nonbiological parent raising a child as his or her own. We can learn a lot from the love demonstrated by everyone involved in these historic stories.

ALL OF GOD'S CHILDREN HAVE AN ADOPTION STORY

The Bible has a lot to say about Christ followers being children of God. John 1:12 says, "Yet to all who did receive him, to those who believed in his name, He gave the right to become children of God." One of my favorite verses says, "See what great love the Father has lavished on us, that we should be called children of God! And that is what we are!" (1 John 3:1a). The Bible also speaks of God adopting us as His children. Romans 8:15 says we receive the Spirit of adoption. Ephesians 1:5 says that God predestined us for adoption to sonship through Jesus Christ. While many translations use the word "predestined," the New Living Translation says that "God decided in advance to adopt us into his own family by bringing us to himself through Jesus Christ. This is what he wanted to do, and it gave him great pleasure." This verse is so powerful!

Yes, adoption is near and dear to God's heart. First, He has made a way for us to be adopted by Him, to become His children. Second, He makes a way for adoption to take place when a child or children cannot be cared for by biological parents. Like the apostle Paul wrote in the book of Ephesians about God, I too can say I wanted to adopt, and it has brought me great pleasure to do so. While adoption was not God's primary plan for families on earth, and there is great sadness and other challenges that can accompany adoption (with the wounds of the children often overlooked), love truly can help overcome these hardships. It's only one part of the equation, but it's a mighty important part.

WHAT IS LOVE?

The founder of Grace Based Families, Tim Kimmel, defines love this way: "Love is the commitment of my will to your needs and best interests, regardless of the cost."[4] Love is selfless and secure. Love is grace and justice. Love is apologizing and forgiving. Love is extending grace to others and yourself when you mess up . . . and you will mess up. Love can best be summed up by sharing the words of 1 Corinthians 13:4–8a:

> Love is patient, love is kind. It does not envy, it does not boast, it is not proud. It does not dishonor others, it is not self-seeking, it is not easily angered, it keeps no record of wrongs. Love does not delight in evil but rejoices with the truth. It always protects, always trusts, always hopes, always perseveres. Love never fails.

Only the love of the Lord truly never fails. God demonstrated His own love for us in that while we were still sinners, Christ died for us.[5] Jesus is the greatest gift of all. It is only because of the love our heavenly Father has for us that we are able to love others. We desperately need Him to sustain us in this parenting journey. Time and again, I go back to the words of affirmation found in the Bible that remind me of who I am and whose I am. Just as we speak loving and kind words over our children, we need to be reminded of them ourselves. We are all fearfully and wonderfully made![6]

More important than any other kind of support, we must rely on the Lord as our main source of strength. Our children will pick up on this and often emulate us. My children have learned that when I am the most overwhelmed or stressed out as a parent, I start to sing. Often, I sing hymns, but I went through a phase when I would just start singing the chorus to Carrie Underwood's "Jesus, Take the Wheel." One day, my daughter was becoming frustrated with something, and she raised her hands as if in praise and exclaimed, "Jesus, take the wheel!" I need Jesus to be in charge and in control every minute of every day. We simply cannot do this parenting thing on our own. Make time (both solo and with your children) to read the Bible and pray. Take your children to church. I understand some of you readers have children with special needs that make going to church challenging, but if there is any way possible, try to make it happen. This might mean driving farther away from home to a church that prioritizes adoption and special needs children. It might mean volunteering more in your child's class to teach other leaders how to best assist your child. It might mean recruiting a team of volunteers to rotate being with your child in his or her class. It might get discouraging, but please don't give up. Our children need the Lord every bit as much as we do.

As a two-year-old, my son would often say, "Hold you, Mama!" when he wanted to be held. His tone of voice when making the request varied from sweet to frantic, depending on the circumstances. Regardless, in those moments, he needed attention, comfort, and love. We're the same way—we can and should go to Jesus asking to be held, in whatever way we can ask and in whatever raw and authentic way we are asking for Him to be with us. He'll never fail us.

In conclusion, I'd like to share one more song-related story. My husband takes our daughter to school each morning. Their routine is to listen to praise and worship music on the way. For a long stretch of time, one of their favorite songs was "Love God, Love People" by Danny Gokey. If you're not familiar with that song, the title words are repeated throughout the song. That was our daughter's time to shine—she had a solo each and every time as she shouted the refrain "LOVE GOD, LOVE PEOPLE." These four words have a significant amount of meaning.

Matthew 22:37–39 states that Jesus said, "'Love the Lord your God with all your heart and with all your soul and with all your mind.' This is the first and greatest commandment. And the second is like it: 'Love your neighbor as yourself.'" The number varies based on the translation, but the word *love* is used hundreds of times in the Bible. First Corinthians 13:13 says that faith, hope, and love remain, "But the greatest of these is love." First John 4:8 says that God is love! Love is the heartbeat of the gospel of Jesus Christ, and it should be the heartbeat of the home. Loving the children who come to us through adoption is not always easy, but it is always worth it. We pray that as you apply the five love languages with your children, your love for them—and their love for you—will only continue to deepen.

Resources

Blogs

Christian Alliance for Orphans (cafo.org/blog/)

Lifetime Christian Adoption (lifetimechristianadoption.com/blog/)

Books *(for adults)*

Adopted for Life by Russell Moore

So You Want to Adopt . . . Now What? by Ruth Graham and Sara Dormon

The Connected Child by Karyn Purvis

The Connected Parent by Karyn Purvis and Lisa Qualls

The Primal Wound: Understanding the Adopted Child by Nancy Newton Verrier

The 5 Love Languages: The Secret to Love That Lasts by Gary Chapman

The 5 Love Languages of Children: The Secret to Loving Children Effectively by Gary Chapman and Ross Campbell

Wait No More: One Family's Amazing Adoption Journey by Kelly and John Rosati

Books (for children)

A Perfect Pet for Peyton by Gary Chapman and Rick Osborne

God Gave Us You by Lisa Tawn Bergren

I Wished for You: An Adoption Story for Kids by Marianne Richmond

The Adoption Tree by Kimberly James

Yes, I'm Adopted! by Sharlie Zinniger

Conferences

CAFO Summit (Christian Alliance for Orphans)

Hope for the Journey (Show Hope)

Replanted Conference (Replanted)

Rooted in Love (Lifeline Children's Services)

Counseling Searches

American Association of Christian Counselors (https://connect .aacc.net/?search_type=distance)

Focus on the Family (www.focusonthefamily.com/get-help/ counseling-services-and-referrals/)

Interventions

Parent Child Interaction Therapy (www.pcit.org)

Play Therapy (https://www.a4pt.org)

TBRI: Trust-Based Relational Intervention (child.tcu.edu)

Theraplay (https://theraplay.org)

Trauma-Focused Cognitive Behavioral Therapy (www.tfcbt.org)

Ministries

Christian Alliance for Orphans (www.cafo.org)

Lifeline Children's Services (www.lifelinechild.org)

Nightlight Christian Adoptions (www.nightlight.org)

Replanted (www.replantedministry.org)

Show Hope (www.showhope.org)

Podcasts

Nightlight Christian Adoptions has a list of ten compelling podcasts (www.nightlight.org/2020/07/ten-compelling-podcasts-about-foster-care-and-adoption/)

Acknowledgments

From Dr. Laurel Shaler:

First and foremost, I would like to thank my Lord and Savior, Jesus Christ, for saving a wretch like me. Second, I am eternally grateful for the opportunity to collaborate with the esteemed Dr. Gary Chapman on this important project. I would also like to thank my husband of over two decades. Nick, you said you would support me in this endeavor, and you have certainly lived up to your promise. Thank you! I love you and our children dearly. I also want to acknowledge my parents, David (1950–2020) and Janeen Stephens. I learned the most about how to be a loving parent from them. Dear Mama, I love you! I also want to say thank you to all my family (especially my three sisters) and friends (too many to name!) who have supported us on our adoption journey. Finally, I would like to give a huge THANK YOU to all who willingly shared their adoption stories. Your contributions are invaluable and helped make this book possible. Gloria in Deo!

From Dr. Gary Chapman:

I want to express my sincere gratitude for the opportunity to work with Dr. Laurel Shaler on this book. Her own experience as an adoptive parent and her academic credentials make her the perfect coauthor for a book dedicated to helping adoptive parents effectively love their children. I also want to thank the editorial team at Moody Publishers for their excellent work in fine-tuning our manuscript.

Notes

Chapter 1: Loving Intentionally

1. "Trends in U.S. Adoptions: 2010–2019," Child Welfare Information Gateway, April 2022, https://www.childwelfare.gov/pubPDFs/adopted2010_19.pdf.
2. Ibid.
3. Ruth Graham and Sara Dormon, *So You Want to Adopt . . . Now What?: A Practical Guide for Navigating the Adoption Process* (Ventura, CA: Regal Books, 2006), 21.
4. Ibid., 29.
5. Genesis 1:28.
6. Nancy Newton Verrier, *The Primal Wound: Understanding the Adopted Child* (Baltimore: Gateway Press, 1993), 53.
7. Gregory C. Keck and Regina M. Kupecky, *Parenting the Hurt Child: Helping Adoptive Families Heal and Grow* (Colorado Springs: Pinon Press, 2002), 215.
8. Ibid., 217.

Chapter 2: Why *This* Book?

1. Gary Chapman, *The 5 Love Languages: The Secret to Love That Lasts* (Chicago: Northfield Publishing, 2015).
2. Gary Chapman and Ross Campbell, *The 5 Love Languages of Children: The Secret to Loving Children Effectively* (Chicago: Northfield Publishing, 2012).
3. Brandy Leyva, "Breakout Session," Replanted Conference, 2022.

Chapter 3: When You Don't "Feel the Love"

1. Vanderbilt University Medical Center, "Standardizing Care Improves Outcomes for Infants Born with Neonatal Abstinence Syndrome," *VUMC Reporter*, April 15, 2016, https://news.vumc.org/2016/04/15/standardizing-care-improves-outcomes-for/.
2. Ministry of Children and Family Development Vancouver Region, "Baby Steps: Caring for Babies with Prenatal Substance Exposure," https://www2.gov.bc.ca/assets/gov/family-and-social-supports/foster-parenting/baby_steps_caring_babies_prenatal_substance_exposure.pdf.
3. Susan Caughman and Isolde Motley, *You Can Adopt: An Adoptive Families Guide* (New York: Ballantine Books, 2009), 201.
4. Sarah L. Mott et al., "Depression and Anxiety among Postpartum and Adoptive Mothers," *Archives of Women's Mental Health*, July 3, 2011, 335–343. https://link.springer.com/article/10.1007/s00737-011-0227-1.
5. Ibid.
6. Tim Kimmel, *Grace Based Parenting: Set Your Family Free,* (Nashville: Thomas Nelson, 2004), 65.
7. Russell Moore, *Adopted for Life: The Priority of Adoption for Christian Families and Churches* (Wheaton, IL: Crossway, 2015), 95.
8. Wendy Kittlitz, "Attachment: What Adoptive Families Need to Know," Focus on the Family, https://www.focusonthefamily.ca/content/attachment-what-adoptive-families-need-to-know.
9. Texas Christian University, "TBRI," "What Is It?," College of Science and Engineering, https://child.tcu.edu/about-us/tbri/#sthash.IcCWEXnh.dpbs.

Chapter 4: Attachment and Reactions

1. Laurel Shaler, *Relational Reset: Unlearning the Habits That Hold You Back* (Chicago: Moody Publishers, 2019).
2. Ibid., 101–103.
3. Cindy Lee, "Breakout Session," Replanted Conference, 2022.
4. Ibid.
5. Daniel Amen, "Child Psychiatry," Amen Clinics, https://www.amenclinics.com/conditions/child-psychiatry.

6. Daniel J. Siegel and Tina P. Bryson, *The Whole-Brain Child: 12 Revolutionary Strategies to Nurture Your Child's Developing Mind* (New York: Bantam Books, 2011), 15.

7. Ibid., 15–16.

8. Ibid.

9. "Trauma: It's More Than Just 'Fight or Flight,'" PTSD UK, https://www.ptsduk.org/its-so-much-more-than-just-fight-or-flight/.

10. Ibid.

11. Walter Cannon, *Bodily Changes in Pain, Hunger, Fear, and Rage: An Account of Recent Researches into the Function of Emotional Excitement* (New York: D. Appleton & Co., 1925).

12. Carmit Katz et al., "Beyond Fight, Flight, and Freeze: Towards a New Conceptualization of Peritraumatic Responses to Child Sexual Abuse Based on Retrospective Accounts of Adult Survivors," *Child Abuse & Neglect*, February 2021, https://www.sciencedirect.com/science/article/abs/pii/S0145213420305603.

13. "Trauma," PTSD UK.

14. Ibid.

15. Ibid.

16. C. Katz and Z. Barnetz, "The Behavior Patterns of Abused Children as Described in Their Testimonies," *Child Abuse & Neglect* 38, no. 6 (June 2014): 1033–40, http://dx.doi.org/10.1016/j.chiabu.2013.08.006.

17. Adoption Triad, "Resources for Children with Fetal Alcohol Spectrum Disorder," September 2019, https://www.childwelfare.gov/news-events/adoptiontriad/editions/sep2019/.

18. Centers for Disease Control and Prevention, "Fetal Alcohol Spectrum Disorders (FASDs)," https://www.cdc.gov/ncbddd/fasd/facts.html.

19. Ibid.

20. Ibid.

21. American Psychological Association, *Diagnostic and Statistical Manual of Mental Disorders, Fifth Edition: DSM-5* (Washington, DC: American Psychiatric Publishing, 2013), 265–68.

22. Ibid.

23. M. Miranda, E. Molla, and E. Tadros, "Implications of Foster Care on Attachment: A Literature Review," *Family Journal*, March 5, 2019, https://www.researchgate.net/publication/331550879_Implications_of_Foster_Care_on_Attachment_A_Literature_Review.

24. "What Is the Circle of Security? Developing Specific Relationship Capacities," Circle of Security International, https://www.circleof securityinternational.com/circle-of-security-model/what-is-the-circle-of-security/.

25. L. Barone, F. Lionetti, and J. Green, "A Matter of Attachment? How Adoptive Parents Foster Post-Institutionalized Children's Social and Emotional Adjustment," *Attachment and Human Development* 19, no. 4 (2017): 323–39, https://doi.org/10.1080/14616734.2017.130 6714.

26. Ibid.

Chapter 5: Acts of Service

1. Matthew 20:28.

Chapter 6: Gifts

1. Angela K., "The Birthday Blues and Adopted Kids," Rainbow Kids, April 14, 2016, https://www.rainbowkids.com/adoption-stories/the-birthday-blues-and-adopted-kids-1604.

2. Ibid.

3. Ibid.

4. Katherine B. Hanniball et al., "Does Helping Promote Well-Being in At-Risk Youth and Ex-Offender Samples?," *Journal of Experimental Social Psychology*, May 2019, 307–17.

Chapter 7: Physical Touch

1. Gary Chapman and Ross Campbell, *The 5 Love Languages of Children: The Secret to Loving Children Effectively* (Chicago: Northfield Publishing, 2012), 29.

2. "Why Hugging Is Actually Good for Your Health," Cleveland Clinic, October 21, 2020, https://health.clevelandclinic.org/why-hugging-is-actually-good-for-your-health-video/.

3. Gregory C. Keck and Regina M. Kupecky, *Parenting the Hurt Child: Helping Adoptive Families Heal and Grow* (Colorado Springs: Pinon Press, 2002), 86.

4. Ibid., 87.

5. Emmelie Pickett, "25 Creative Ways to Give Healthy Touch," Karyn Purvis Institute of Child Development, https://child.tcu.edu/blog_25-creative-ways-to-give-healthy touch/#sthash.Nzv8avtk.49Nyfdk5.dpbs.

6. C. Keysers and V. Gazzola, "Hebbian Learning and Predictive Mirror Neurons for Actions, Sensations and Emotions," *Philosophical Transactions of the Royal Society of London*, June 5, 2014, 1–11.

7. "Parenting a Child or Youth Who Has Been Sexually Abused: A Guide for Foster and Adoptive Parents," Child Welfare Information Gateway, December 2018, https://www.childwelfare.gov/pubpdfs/f_abused.pdf.

8. Ibid.

9. Ibid.

10. "Emotional Regulation: Sensory Processing Disorder," Holt International, June 7, 2011, https://www.holtinternational.org/emotional-regulation-sensory-processing-disorder-2/.

11. M. G. Scott et al., "A Mother's Touch: Preschool-Aged Children Are Regulated by Positive Maternal Touch," *Developmental Psychobiology*, February 22, 2022, 1–12.

12. D. Ellingsen et al., "The Neurobiology Shaping Affective Touch: Expectation, Motivation, and Meaning in the Multisensory Context," *Frontiers in Psychology*, January 6, 2016, 1–16.

Chapter 8: Quality Time

1. Positive Parenting Solutions, "How as Little as 20 Minutes a Day Can Change Your Whole Year: 3 Quality-Time Tips for Toddlers to Teens," Positive Parenting Solutions, https://www.positiveparentingsolutions.com/parenting/how-as-little-as-20-minutes-a-day-can-change-your-whole-year.

2. Ibid.

3. "Quality Time," 5 Love Languages, https://5lovelanguages.com/learn.

4. American Psychological Association, "Metacommunication," https://dictionary.apa.org/metacommunication.

5. Tim Kimmel, *Grace Based Parenting: Set Your Family Free* (Nashville: Thomas Nelson, 2004), 49.
6. Matthew 6:21.

Chapter 9: Words of Affirmation
1. Anita Knight Kuhnley, *The Mister Rogers Effect: 7 Secrets to Bringing Out the Best in Yourself and Others from America's Beloved Neighbor* (Ada, MI: Baker Books, 2020), 180.
2. Proverbs 18:21.
3. Luke 6:45.

Chapter 10: Challenging Circumstances
1. Abigail Lindner, "Single Parent Adoption: The Process and Experience of Adopting Unpartnered," National Council for Adoption, August 31, 2021, https://adoptioncouncil.org/publications/single-parent-adoption-the-process-and-experience-of-adopting-unpartnered/.
2. Ibid.
3. Gary Chapman and Ron Deal, *Building Love Together in Blended Families: The 5 Love Languages and Becoming Stepfamily Smart* (Chicago: Northfield Publishing, 2020).
4. Allon Kalisher, Jennah Gosciak, and Jill Spielfogel, "The Multiethnic Placement Act 25 Years Later: Trends in Adoption and Transracial Adoption," US Department of Health and Human Services, December 2020, https://aspe.hhs.gov/sites/default/files/private/pdf/264526/MEPA-Data-report.pdf.

Chapter 11: All About Siblings
1. "What to Know about Birth Order," Grow by WebMD, https://www.webmd.com/parenting/what-to-know-about-birth-order.
2. Ibid.
3. Susan Caughman and Isolde Motley, *You Can Adopt: An Adoptive Families Guide* (New York: Ballantine Books, 2009), 252.

Chapter 12: Adoption Support
1. "Guidelines," Association for Play Therapy, https://www.a4pt.org/page/ClarifyingUseofPT.

2. Ibid.
3. "What Is PCIT?," Parent Child Interaction Therapy, https://www
   .pcit.org/what-is-pcit-for-professionals.html.
4. Ibid.
5. Carl R. Rogers, "The Necessary and Sufficient Conditions of
   Therapeutic Personality Change," *Journal of Consulting Psychology*,
   June 6, 1956, 95–103.
6. Ibid.

Chapter 13: Faith Matters

1. Exodus 2:1–10.
2. Esther 2:1–20 NLT.
3. Esther 4:14 NLT.
4. Tim Kimmel, *Grace Based Parenting: Set Your Family Free* (Nashville:
   Thomas Nelson, 2004), 52.
5. Romans 5:8.
6. Psalm 139:14.

Simple ways to strengthen relationships.

TAKE THE LOVE LANGUAGE® QUIZ

DOWNLOAD FREE RESOURCES AND STUDY GUIDES

BROWSE THE LOVE LANGUAGE® GIFT GUIDE

SUBSCRIBE TO PODCASTS

SHOP THE STORE

SIGN UP FOR THE NEWSLETTER

Visit www.5lovelanguages.com

TO GET YOUR FAMILY CLOSE, YOU HAVE TO GET IT TALKING.

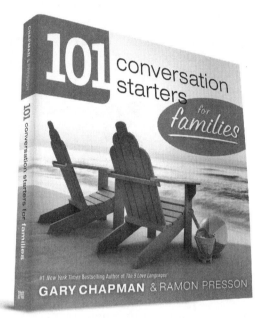

One of the signs of a healthy family is open and meaningful conversation. But it's not always easy to get your kids talking. *101 Conversation Starters for Families* is an excellent resource, providing just the right blend of fun and thought-provoking questions.

Also available as an eBook